"COMMON SENSE-THE WAY BACK"

BY FELTON WILLIAMSON JR   AKA "TOBY"

"THESE ARE THE TIMES THAT TRY MEN'S SOULS"
THOMAS PAINE, 1776

THOMAS PAINE

SPEAKS FOR LIBERTY

"COMMON SENSE –THE WAY BACK"

Felton Williamson Jr
Commerce, Georgia
http://commonsense21c.com/

12/17/2011 REVISION

ISBN # 9781449543884
EAN-13   9 781449 543884

PRINTED IN THE UNITED STATES OF AMERICA

TABLE OF CONTENTS

CAPITALISM – A BELATED OBITUARY

Pure capitalism has never existed; it is similar to absolute zero in physics. Like absolute zero, Capitalism has been approached but never actually achieved. The United States Constitution, perhaps, produced the closest thing to Capitalism that the world has ever seen. Even though our Capitalism was flawed, it produced unprecedented prosperity and undreamed of technological achievements. Under a mostly Capitalistic society, the steam engine, whose design dated back over 1000 years before the emergence of Capitalism, became a practical labor saving tool. The steam engine and subsequent innovation improved man's productivity and created a prosperity and well-being for the average citizen that is unique in all recorded history. Entrepreneurs exploited innovation and created the industries that increased our productivity and reduced the cost of almost all goods and services required to sustain and enhance our lives. Envy of the wealth accumulated by these entrepreneurs caused society to move away from its capitalistic roots.

In 1888, the Congress created the ICC (Interstate Commerce Commission). Two years later the Congress passed the Sherman Antitrust Act. Capitalism became quite ill; contracting a fatal disease after Congress enacted these two laws. Around the turn-of-the-century the Wannabe Tyrants enforced and strengthened these laws, and Capitalism lay down on its death bed, never to rise again. On its death bed, Capitalism was slowly replaced by Cronyism. Few even acknowledged its demise when Capitalism passed away in the mid-1930s. Capitalism had been completely replaced by Cronyism.

Even though Capitalism has passed away, Wannabe Tyrants ignored its demise and continued to blame the corpse for the economic failures of Cronyism. Cronyism, continued to degenerate into Tyranny. Cronyism is simply the transition between Capitalism and Tyranny. The evolution of cronyism to tyranny is almost complete. How did it happen? Can Capitalism be resurrected? Read this book.

FOREWORD

"COMMON SENSE – THE WAY BACK" is a condensed version of the author's first book, "21st CENTURY COMMON SENSE". The original book contained considerable proof and descriptions of the consequences of 5 of the "WANNABE PEERS'" "SHOWCASE PROGRAMS". To highlight the danger to our Republic, detailed descriptions of how 20th Century dictators came to power was included. The chapter on how 20th Century dictators came to power and much of the details of the consequences of the 5 "SHOWCASE PROGRAMS" have been removed in this book in the interest of brevity and simplicity. If the reader accepts the basic premise that **freedom equals prosperity and tyranny equals poverty,** there is no need to wade through such a detailed proof or the description of how the 20th Century dictators came to power.

The 5 "SHOWCASE" programs are:
- THE SHERMAN ANTITRUST ACT
- THE BUREAUCRACY – INTERSTATE COMMERCE COMMISSION
- INFLATION
- EARMARKS
- THE INCOME TAX

Those who are interested in reviewing the more detailed proof and the research that led to these 2 books may go to the website "commonsense21c.com for a complete list of that research on the "BIBLIOGRAPHY" page. Much of the research was done on the internet and each website listed is a link to that website. Of course you could just read my book.

The loss of individual freedom has brought America to the brink of the final economic crisis that will result in a Totalitarian government. The only thing that this old man could do to try to save his country was to write the books, "21st CENTURY COMMON SENSE" and "COMMON SENSE – THE WAY BACK". Both books are attempts to rally our citizens to the cause of freedom and prosperity. Will you choose **freedom and prosperity** over the "WANNABE PEERS'" stale promises of unearned wealth and security?

If the last vestiges of Capitalism (individual freedom) in the United States are destroyed, there will be no savior. The United States saved the world from the evils of Totalitarian government in WORLD WAR II but there will be no one to save us. The world will sink back into the evil of the middle ages.

Years of deterioration of America's basic education has resulted in a majority of our citizens' failure to understand individual freedom and the role that individual freedom plays in the creation of wealth and prosperity. This book provides the historic proof that creation of wealth and your prosperity was impossible until the "divine rights of the King" was discarded in favor of individual freedom. Individual freedom was the indispensible ingredient in the "Industrial Revolution" and the driving force of the American Revolution.

The bibliography websites are listed because of the facts contained there, not the analysis and conclusions of those facts. The conclusions on the bibliography websites do not always agree with the conclusions made in this book. Of course you are free to decide whose interpretation of the facts is correct.

The purpose of the book is to try to rewrite Mr. Paine's "COMMON SENSE" as he would write it today, with the advantage of over 200 years of history unavailable to him in 1776. That is quite an ambition for a senile old man. Was I successful? Please email your comments, along with the proof of any disagreements or fallacies you find to tobywil3@yahoo.com. After all, I may be old but I am not too old to learn.

I have to thank my soul mate of over 50 years, B. Francine Williamson, and our son Felton III (aka Lou) for their encouragement, comments and proof reading the manuscript. Without their help and encouragement there would be no book and you would have saved a few bucks.

GOD BLESS AMERICA!

CHAPTER ONE

"21ST CENTURY COMMON SENSE"

Over two hundred years have passed since we won our freedom from King George III. We are again standing on "Lexington Green[25]" with our freedom in peril, just as it was when the "Minutemen" faced the British Regulars on the fateful day of April 19, 1775; the day the "shot heard around the world" started the American Revolution.

The threat is no longer the "**DIVINE RIGHT OF KINGS**"[30] enforced by King George III and his "Peers". Today the danger is accepting the "Wannabe Peers'" promise of security and unearned wealth.

In 1776, the Colonies stood at the crossroads between FREEDOM and the tyranny of servitude to King George III. On

January 10, 1776, faced with this choice of freedom or tyranny, Thomas Paine[47] published the pamphlet "COMMON SENSE"[47]. The pamphlet was America's first and most important bestselling book. Thomas Paine's "COMMON SENSE" inspired the Colonists to choose freedom and prosperity.

For over 100 years the "Wannabe Peers" (politicians lusting after the power and prestige enjoyed by King George III's "Peers") have used false promises of security and unearned wealth to regain that power and prestige. The "Wannabe Peers'" campaign has been very successful. Our "Founding Fathers" would be appalled at the loss of freedom and the power wielded by the bureaucrats and "Wannabe Peers" of today.

Instead of the British Regulars that advanced on "Lexington Green", we are faced with hordes of bureaucrats. Make no mistake about it; the bureaucrat's weapons are just as effective against you as the British Regular's muskets were on Lexington Green.

TYRANT'S HATCHET MAN
THE BUREAUCRAT

common sense21c.com

The "Wannabe Peers" program has created a system that is almost as oppressive as the system that caused the original Minutemen to rebel. Unless the present trend is reversed, we will soon live under a Totalitarian government.

The choice must be made now; it will soon be too late. Will you choose the freedom created by the "Founding Fathers" or will you be seduced by the "Wannabe Peers'" false promises of security and unearned wealth?

In Thomas Paine's time, the prevailing form of government was the "Kingdom". Though nomenclature varied with the location, there was little difference between the "Kingdoms". Some "Kingdoms", such as England, placed some restrictions on the absolute power of the "King". Any restrictions on the absolute power of the "King" increased individual freedom and the most prosperous of these "Kingdoms" were those with the most individual freedom. The "Kingdom" (Totalitarian) form of government was considered normal and was accepted by the "Commons"; few recognized that there was an alternative. Mr. Paine's "COMMON SENSE" provided that alternative.

"COMMON SENSE" was a clear, logical, easily understood and irrefutable defense of individual freedom. Eloquent and inspiring, Mr. Paine's condemnation of England's near "Totalitarian" Kingdom and the promotion of individual liberty inspired the Colonists to fight and win independence.

The arguments in "COMMON SENSE" are as valid today as they were when the pamphlet was written over 200 years ago and the "Kingdom" form of government has been thoroughly discredited. Today, few dare to openly advocate the "Kingdom" form of government.

Once free of tyranny, the Colonists established a government that guaranteed individual freedom (for citizens) including the right to create and enjoy wealth. Perhaps the only flaw was failure to eliminate the institution of slavery. The result was over 200 years of prosperity and technological achievement that is unequalled in the history of the world. In less than 200 years, the state of the art of transportation changed from horses and sailing ships to supersonic aircraft, nuclear submarines and automobiles travelling on super highways. Innovation, featuring the use of mechanical energy to replace "muscle power", provided huge increases in individual productivity. The reduction in labor and resources required to produce the necessities of life freed those resources to produce luxuries for the masses. Increases in individual productivity created prosperity undreamed of when our Constitution was adopted. Luxuries, unheard of in King George III's day, became commonplace. The standard of living of each generation improved and that increasing prosperity continued into the Twenty-First Century.

When America won independence, the source of power changed from the "King" to the ballot box. With the change in the source of power, a new class of citizen emerged-the "Wannabe Peers". The "Wannabe Peers" lusted after the power and prestige that the British "Peers" had enjoyed under King George III.

"Wannabe Peers" wanted to use the government's monopoly on force to control the "Commons" (creators of wealth) and punish those who resisted their benevolent coercion.

The "Wannabe Peers" realized that new strategic and tactical initiatives would be required to regain the power that the British "Peers" enjoyed under the "King".

Tactics and strategy were devised to use the ballot box to regain their lost power. Realizing that their natural constituency was the desperate and poverty stricken, the "Wannabe Peers" knew that general prosperity and economic stability were not in their best interest. Both Hitler and Mussolini required severe economic crises to achieve their coup.

The "Wannabe Peers" would claim the moral "high ground" and proclaim that the purpose of their agenda was to aid the unfortunate, provide security, improve the environment (added later), correct social injustices, and prevent exploitation of the consumer by the producer. However, the **real** purpose of their agenda was to regain the power and prestige possessed by King George III's "Peers".

Prosperity is the most formidable obstacle to the "Wannabe Peers'" increasing their power. Even though the "Wannabe Peers" claim to aid the "unfortunate", almost every item in their agenda destroys wealth.

This destruction of wealth has the greatest effect on the standard of living of the "unfortunate" and forces more people below the poverty level. The net result has been an increase in the "Wannabe Peers'" constituency!

A more detailed discussion of the successes of the "Wannabe Peers'" agenda is presented later. Briefly, the "Wannabe Peers" successes are:

- Earmarks that in 2008 removed $16.5 billion dollars from the economy.
- Meddling in the relationship between the employer and employee has virtually bankrupted the American automobile industry, increased everyone's cost of living (inflation) and resulted in government enforced racial discrimination. The meddling has allowed the "Wannabe Peers" to obtain political support for the favors provided to the "Pawns" (special interests).

- Rules and regulations restricting the harvesting of natural resources have made us dependent on those hostile to freedom for our energy, resulting in the squandering of our wealth and preventing creation of wealth in our country.
- An Income Tax Code too complicated to understand or comply with. It has the capacity to make almost anyone a criminal, requiring only a close enough investigation to find the non-compliance. This has huge potential to stifle political dissent.
- Taxing productivity (income tax) can only have the effect of limiting the creation of wealth.
- Non objective antitrust laws that are interpreted by political expediency and change with the judge and political pressure. These laws punish productivity, reward mediocrity and stifle innovation.
- Creating a bureaucracy that acts as legislator, plaintive, police, prosecutor, judge, and jury. Enforcing its rules and regulations by reversing the basic tenet of our law that one is innocent until proven guilty. (Examples? The IRS and EPA come to mind. The bureaucracy has a huge potential to silence political dissent).
- Rules and regulations involving health care and drugs that have driven the cost of health care to the ridiculous extreme by catering to special interests.
- A justice system that allows for years of incarceration (innocent until proven guilty?) prior to trial and requires one to expend one's life savings for defense. The reward for innocence? Possibly an apology and loss of one's life savings.
- Destruction of the Constitution by appointing judges that legislate from the bench, giving the "Wannabe Peers" the power to create laws that could not be passed by the Legislature.
- Bureaucracies require "environmental impact statements" that delay projects for years and increase the cost of innovation, preventing the creation of wealth. The same bureaucracy has the power to create and enforce new rules and regulations that wreak havoc on the economy with no regard for the consequences of their actions.
- Behavior control laws that create victimless crimes and "controlled substance" laws that are no more effective than the "prohibition laws" of the early Twentieth Century. The laws provide a source of income for the criminal element, dislocate

5

the economy and fail to protect the public from erratic behavior caused by the use of dangerous drugs.

The "common enemy" is a necessity for those who would usurp your liberty and the "Wannabe Peers" selected the **"Rich"** (the creator of wealth and Mr. Paine's "Commons") as the common enemy. Hitler's enemies were the Jews and Communists, Mussolini's enemies were the Communists and Socialists.

The "Wannabe Peers'" "preponderance of propaganda" campaign would dwell on the positive results they promised for their agenda and ignore the negative results that would actually occur.

The "Wannabe Peers" were able to make very little progress until the late 19TH Century. Their first big success was the Sherman Antitrust act[24], a non objective law that could be applied against any successful "Commons", (creators of wealth). It provided the tool to influence, if not control, the "Commons". The Sherman Antitrust Act was enacted in 1890. With this first weapon firmly in place, the second hundred years rewarded the "Wannabe Peers" with compounding successes. They are very close to completely dismantling the great economic engine that the "Founding Fathers" created. America's first "retro-generation" will soon be a reality. When the "standard of living" declines for a generation, that generation is a "retro generation". We may already be members of the first American "retro-generation.

The affects of the success of the "Wannabe Peers'" agenda is very close to creating the economic crisis that is required to achieve the coup that creates a Dictator. Today, we are all standing on the 21ST Century "Lexington Green"[25] and unless we take immediate action, King George III and his henchman "Peers" will have the last laugh.

The "Wannabe Peers" tell us we should surrender our freedom (and our prosperity) for the promise of security and unearned wealth. BENJAMIN FRANKLIN'S[19] eloquent quote "**they who would give up an essential liberty for temporary security, deserve neither liberty or security**" would seem to settle the question of swapping freedom for security.

The use of the government to provide advantage of one citizen over another is a fleeting proposition that shifts with the political fortunes resulting in the loss of freedom for all concerned. The only lasting result is the enhanced power of the "Wannabe Peers". Mr. Paine could never have conceived of a people, once free, surrendering their liberty for promises of security, unearned wealth or political advantage over their neighbor.

Mr. Paine's "COMMON SENSE" divided the citizens of England into three Classes:

- The "King"
- The "Peers"
- The "Commons"

Of course, the "King" is not a factor in America now, but the "Kings" (goes by many names) still control much of the world. The "Peers", or aristocrats, who held the position of authority at the "King's" pleasure, are long gone. The English "Peers" have been replaced by politicians, "Wannabe Peers", using the ballot box to try to obtain the power and prestige formally bestowed by King George III on his "Peers".

To update Mr. Paine's citizens list to the Twenty-First Century, it is necessary to add one Class, the "Pawns". This terminology will be used throughout this book. The use of the common labels, Communist, Socialist, Fascist, "Conservatives" and "Liberals" are just part of the confusion. These labels are simply different names for tyranny. All those common labels are used to describe politicians who covet your freedom. Ayn Rand, perhaps history's greatest champion of Capitalism, was asked if she were a Conservative. "No" was her answer. She said she was a "radical for Capitalism", that there was nothing left to conserve.

The fallacy that Communism, Socialism and Fascism were at different ends of the political spectrum was used very successfully by both Hitler and Mussolini in their quest for power. The political spectrum consists of individual freedom on the extreme right and the various forms of slavery (Communism, Socialism and Fascism) on the extreme left. Liberals on the left-center and Conservatives on the right-center define the "mixed economy" that spans the area between freedom and slavery. The only difference between Communism, Socialism and Fascism is the rhetoric, the arguments and personality of the Dictator. The "mixed economy" may only be the transition period between freedom and slavery.

THE POLITICAL SPECTRUM

LEFT (TYRANTS)
POVERTY &
DESPAIR

LEFT CENTER
(PROGRESSIVES)

RIGHT CENTER
(RINOS)

RIGHT (PATRIOT)
PROSPERITY &
FREEDOM

Commonsense21c.com

The "King" had virtually unlimited power and delegated that power to the "Peers" for the oppression of the "Commons" (producers). The wealth extracted by the oppression of the "Commons" maintained the "Peers" and the "King" in what passed for luxury in the pre-industrial revolution world. Although in 1776 England, his power was theoretically limited, the "King" could manipulate the system to achieve his purpose.

In Mr. Paine's day, the "Peers" status was determined by birth and maintained at the pleasure of the "King". "Peers" controlled considerable wealth and power so they were easy to identify. There was little or no movement between classes. Not so today. **Any ambitious political psychopath can become a "Wannabe Peer".**

The post-revolution "Wannabe Peers" are the leaders of the groups that seek to control and/or exploit the individual by using the government's monopoly on force. The "Wannabe Peers" are divided into three groups:

The "Power Seeking Wannabe Peers" are those seeking power for power's sake. They want to upgrade themselves into the "Kings" Class. Hitler is a good example of this most dangerous type of "Wannabe Peer". Some may even believe their own propaganda and see themselves as the "savior of the masses".

"Economic Wannabe Peers" try to use the power of the Government to achieve financial advantage. The confiscation of private property and subsequently awarding the property to the "Economic Wannabe Peers" for "economic development" is an excellent example of the successful campaigns by the "Economic Wannabe Peers". Another common objective of the "Economic Wannabe Peers" is to seek to use the power of the government to maintain the "status quo" when innovation threatens to cause them economic damage.

"Behavior Control Wannabe Peers" seeking to use the power of the Government to force their ideas (a limited agenda) on the individual. If they are successful, they will try to expand their agenda. The Eighteenth Amendment, "Prohibition", is an example of their success.

Both the "Economic Wannabe Peers" and the "Behavior Control Wannabe Peers" might be considered "Pawns" because they are the "special interest" the "Power Seeking Wannabe Peers" exploit to obtain power.

Modern "Wannabe Peers" are much more subtle and devious than Mr. Paine's "Peers". Heredity no longer defines one as a "PEER". Today, the "Wannabe Peers" are defined by their actions and the identity as a "Wannabe Peer" is carefully hidden even after obtaining power. For the "Wannabe Peers", the end justifies the means and **they will use any form of deception to obtain power.** After all, no one will surrender their liberty if they know what they are doing. To use the ballot box as a source of power, the "Wannabe Peers" created the new class, the "Pawns".

The "Pawns" are those deceived by the "Wannabe Peers" and believe that the "Wannabe Peers" will provide redistribution of the "Commons'" wealth, or give them a competitive advantage or the means to force their will on the "Commons". The "Pawns" don't realize that they too are surrendering their freedom.

In 1776 England, the "Commons" were the real creators of wealth. It was the "Commons" who actually produced the food, built the ships and produced the wealth required for society to exist. The "Commons" lived on the crumbs they were able to hide from the "Peers" and the rewards received from enlightened "Peers" who realized that incentives could actually increase production much more than the cost of the incentives. Incentives were okay as long as the "Commons" knew their "place".

The "Commons" are still the creators of wealth. The freedom won in the Revolution allowed the "Commons" to create wealth and a standard of living that was inconceivable under the tyranny. For the first time in history, the "Commons", not the "Peers", controlled the majority of wealth.

Since Paine's "COMMON SENSE" was written and the "LAND OF THE FREE AND THE HOME OF THE BRAVE" has won its freedom from England, a middle class has been established. The "Peers" right to initiate force against the "Commons", confiscate their wealth or simply impose their will has been severely limited, but it has not been eliminated. Since Cornwallis surrendered to George Washington, the "Wannabe Peers" have been chipping away at the "Commons" individual rights. The true nature of their agenda is hidden in eloquent dialogue. The "Wannabe Peers" use promises of prosperity, redistribution of wealth, the "Common Good", demonizing an enemy and criminalizing the behavior that the "Behavior Control Wannabe Peers" find objectionable, to gain power. It is interesting to study how both Hitler and Mussolini used these arguments to gain power.

The "Wannabe Peers'" arguments are long on sarcasm, emotion and lies but short on logic and facts. Because of the ineffective defense of our liberty, many of the "Wannabe Peers'" proposals have been enacted and are now public policy. Poor Thomas Paine must be spinning in his grave.

The objective of this book is simply to update Paine's "COMMON SENSE" and apply its principles to the world as it exists today. A word of caution; it is possible to be a "Peer" and a "Common" at the same time. A "Common" who created considerable wealth exploiting a new technology frequently seeks government aid to suppress innovation when they become technologically challenged. Attacks on individual freedom cannot be justified by one's productivity. Yes, life is not "black and white" but shades of gray. But life is gray because the good and bad are mixed. It is the individual's responsibility to separate the good from the bad and discard the bad. Life is hard.

In addition to his writing, Thomas Paine was a mechanical designer. One of his designs was a cast iron bridge conceived to replace wooden bridges that were susceptible to ice damage in the winter. His bridge concepts were never built but were seriously considered both in Europe and America. His writings clearly show the discipline and ability to redefine and simplify problems which are acquired by technical or scientific education.

The engineer uses techniques like "free body diagrams" and "systems analysis" to identify and simplify problems. These techniques also identify and isolate the irrelevant, allowing the engineer to understand and solve complicated problems or predict the performance of a new design. With a little imagination, many of the laws of physics have application to the evaluation of the "Wannabe Peers" proposals. An example is The **First Law Of Thermodynamics,** the law of conservation of energy. It states that **"the energy added to a substance = the change in internal energy + the mechanical energy given out or taken in".** Paraphrased, it says that "energy can be neither created nor destroyed" or **"you can't get something for nothing"**. Rigorously applied, the first law of thermodynamics debunks most of the "Wannabe Peers" proposals.

The engineer, using "System Analysis", simplifies a problem by drawing a circle around the process and using arrows to show input and output. What occurs inside the circle is ignored.

FIG. 1

For instance, to determine efficiency in a heat engine you divide the device's usable output by the heat input and multiply by 100 and you have the device's percent efficiency. No worries about valve timing, compression ratio, rpm or carbon dioxide emissions. You have calculated the efficiency, simply and easily by ignoring the irrelevant information. This tool, when applied to political proposals, enhances and simplifies the evaluation of those proposals. "Wannabe Peers" have no problem proposing violations of the laws of physics or the laws of human nature. They purposely complicate the proposals and predict unlikely, if not impossible results. The "Wannabe Peers" won't apologize when their agenda fails to achieve the promised results. They will just accept the surrender of some of your freedom and spin another "fairy tale".System analysis techniques will make the evaluation and debunking of the "Wannabe Peers" proposals easy and help you understand their real objective. To illustrate, let's see how these tools might have been used to avoid problems resulting from a historic disaster caused by the Government's use of force to violate individual rights. There are many such instances in history. One such program that occurred long ago and has been thoroughly discredited by time is "Prohibition" [1] (the Eighteenth Amendment to the Constitution).The "Wannabe Peers" system analysis is shown in   figure 1.

REAL SYSTEM ANALYSIS OF PROHIBITION

BEFORE PROHIBITION

LEGAL INDUSTRY

TAXES COLLECTED

LEGITIMATE JOBS

ABUSE DISCOURAGED BY VENDORS

ALCOHOL ABUSE

BROKEN FAMILIES

Fig.2

P R O H I B I T I O N

AFTER PROHIBITION

CREATED ILLEGAL INDUSTRY

NO TAXES

HIGH ENFORCEMENT COST

GANGSTERS REPLACED WORKERS

CORRUPTION OF OFFICIALS

VIOLENCE AND EXTORTION

POISON ALCOHOL SOLD

ENCOURAGED ALCOHOL ABUSE

MORE BROKEN FAMILIES

INCREASED ALCOHOL ABUSE

Prohibition resulted in violence, death and disability caused by contaminated alcohol, gun fights in the streets and political corruption, which many say continues in Chicago after over 75 years. The measure failed to stop the use of alcohol (some say the use of alcohol increased during the prohibition years). The failure highlights the difficulty of controlling human behavior by the use of force. Real system analysis is contained in the chart Fig. 2.

The "Wannabe Peers" used the media to saturate the country with the "preponderance of propaganda" filled with lies, sarcasm, and promises of utopia to sell the country on their scheme. The "Prohibition Wannabe Peers" system analysis would have looked like Fig.1 above. The real chart is shown in Fig. 2

With a little logic and reason, Fig. 2 could have been created in 1918, just as easily as today, and the pain and suffering caused by that intrusion on individual freedom avoided.

Before the engineering analysis can begin, data must be collected and evaluated. The data or facts that will be used in the analysis are listed below. Many are common knowledge, but few of us understand the true implications. You may consider some controversial. Each item will be discussed, clarified in detail at the appropriate time.

AYN RAND[3] believed that the primary purpose of the government was to protect the individual from the initiation of physical force and violence, both foreign and domestic. Freedom from the initiation of physical force and violence for all is in the long term best interest of everyone. This statement has much wider application than simply protection from robbery. For instance, the pollution which affects the life and property of others is certainly the initiation of force.

Wealth, unlike energy, can be created, destroyed and consumed. Over time, wealth (except some commodities) will become obsolete or be consumed. Therefore, continuous creation of wealth is necessary to continue life as we know it and benefits the whole of society. In the late 1940's, the government had an advertising campaign with the slogan, **"THE MORE WE PRODUCE, THE BETTER WE LIVE."** It's as true today as it was then.

The principles and facts upon which this book is based are listed below. Historical evidence is offered in the bibliography to validate these principles and later discussion will show how their violation has affected your life.

- The initiation of the use of physical force is incompatible with the creation of wealth.

- Wealth is much easier to consume or destroy than it is to create.
- Wealth must be created before it can be consumed.
- Wealth is the property of the creator of that wealth.
- Creation of wealth is defined as creating or increasing the value of an asset.
- Persecution and harassment of the "Commons" (producer) is not in the best interest of the consumer.
- The ingredients in the recipe for the creation of wealth are freedom, intellectual activity, labor, energy, education, capital investment, a stable government, transportation, ambition and self preservation.
- All "consumable assets" have energy content. Any increase in the cost of energy or decrease in availability of energy increases the cost and restricts the production of "consumable assets" and reduces your standard of living..
- History has shown that the closer a society is to "pure capitalism" the more prosperous that society is.
- The capitalistic society encourages innovation. Innovation is the source of "technology dividend". (The historic growth of the "technology dividend" is discussed in Chapter2.) The book, "AN EMPIRE OF WEALTH" by John Steele Gordon[20] is also an account of how technical innovation created America's wealth. The "technology dividend" is the increase in individual productivity that reduces the amount of effort or material required to produce wealth. An increase in the standard of living requires a corresponding increase in individual productivity.
- The "technology dividend" brings new products to market and enhances our life.
- Money is not wealth. Money is a medium of exchange. It is the creation of wealth that gives money value.
- Control of the supply of the "medium of exchange" (money) is one of the "Wannabe Peers" most prized tools.
- Prices in a free market are controlled by supply and demand. Upon interruption or fear of an interruption of supply, the price will rise.

- Fossil fuels will be the most economical source of energy (assuming no catastrophic interference by the "Wannabe Peers") for at least 200 years. There may be some opportunities for economical harvesting of "alternative energy" due to the terrain, constant winds, or easily available heat below the earth's crust. These situations can provide only a small fraction of the energy necessary to power our economy. However, these will be the exception, not the rule. When amortization of capital investment and intermittent availability of the energy source is considered, there is no economical substitute for fossil fuel. Nuclear power may be an exception. The "Wannabe Peers" want the government to solve a problem that won't exist for over 200 years, yet they ignore imminent problems which offer them no opportunity to increase their power. Who will benefit from this misapplication of capital? The "Wannabe Peers" and their political cronies, of course, and most of us will surely lose.

- Carbon dioxide has not been proven to be the cause of climate change[6]. This fable has been proven only by the preponderance of the propaganda. Computer models which predict climate change based upon increased carbon dioxide do not pass back testing. Do not allow the "Wannabe Peers" to destroy your standard of living on a quest to fight windmills that even Don Quixote would recognize. **There is no issue, today, that has more potential to destroy the economy, push more of the population below the poverty line and allow the "Wannabe Peers" to increase their control over the individual.** Trying to control climate change by controlling carbon dioxide emissions would be like removing the cigarette lighter from your car to increase gas mileage.

- The "technology dividend" continuously reduces the real cost of goods and services.

- Even though the "technology dividend" continuously reduces the **real cost** of goods and services, in a real system, the cost (in currency) of goods (includes gold and other natural resources) and services **increases** due to inflation of the medium of exchange.

- Capitalism requires the continual redeployment of resources as innovation causes obsolescence of facilities and changes the demand for products. Innovation without obsolescence is impossible. This obsolescence is painful. It causes valuable labor skills and production equipment to become worthless.

- Natural resources (oil, coal, iron ore etc.) are potential wealth, just as a weight suspended in air contains potential energy and requires a machine to convert it into useful work. Natural resources require that "Commons" expend effort and capital to convert it into wealth.

- Innovation requires energy. Most of the "technology dividend" involves the use of energy to increase the individual's productivity. Restrict the use of energy and you reduce the individual's productivity and standard of living.

- Even the most prosperous societies have finite assets. Misallocation or restrictions on the use of assets reduces prosperity. Restricting individual freedom is a restriction on the use of an asset. Political deployments of wealth (Earmarks are an example) are usually misapplication of wealth.

- Misallocation of assets reduces prosperity and counteracts the "technology dividend".

- Increasing productivity has the greatest effect on the standard of living of the lowest level of society as it reduces the real cost of the wealth ("consumable assets") necessary for survival. Typically, the lowest level of society expends their total effort to barely survive so any reduction in the cost of survival increases the well-being of that group.

- The primary constituencies of the "Wannabe Peers" are the lower level of society, primarily those dependent on the government aid for survival.

- The composition of their constituency is not lost on the "Wannabe Peers". When the deception is stripped from their agenda, it becomes obvious that almost every item of their agenda will result in either destruction of wealth or restriction on the creation of wealth.

- The "Wannabe Peers" claim the moral high ground. They claim that they are trying to help "those less fortunate", work for the "common good", provide protection from an enemy or protect us from our "vices". Yet, the "Wannabe

Peers'" every proposal limits our liberty, inhibits production and destroys or confiscates wealth.

• A favorite tactic of the "Wannabe Peers" is to vilify a common "enemy" and use the defense against that enemy to obtain popular support. Many times the vilification is the justification for oppression and confiscation of the "enemy's" property.

• Only the individual has rights. Special rights conferred on any group must first be taken away from the individual.

• When an individual's rights are lost, the individual becomes more dependent on the government, thus giving the "Wannabe Peers" more control over the individual's life and property. Loss of rights generally results in an increase in the "Pawn" population and a resulting increase in the "Wannabe Peers" constituency.

• There is no government program, no matter how poorly conceived and implemented, that does not have some positive effects.

• Monopolies can exist only when backed by force.

• "By Right of Conquest" before WWII this pretty much summed up the morality of foreign relations in the world. What this means is that when a nation won a war, that nation had the right to appropriate the territory and wealth of the loser. "By Right of Conquest" is a principle much prized by foreign "Kings" and their henchmen, the "Peers". Of course, usually a nation would trump up some grievances before it attacked its neighbor. But the real cause of most wars was, and still is, the lust for the neighbor's wealth.

• As wealthy and strong as America is, it cannot feed, clothe, shelter and provide health care for the world. Subsidizing the victims of foreign "Kings" and "Peers" cannot provide lasting relief. As long as major portions of the world punish productivity and believe it is easier to confiscate wealth than to create it, poverty will be rampant. "Kings" and "Peers" can destroy and consume wealth much faster than America can create it. It is futile to try to raise the standard of living where ownership of wealth is determined by force.

- America cannot depose the "Kings" and "Peers" who have popular support even though they are causing widespread poverty and injustice.
- Any Totalitarian government (a government totally controlled by the "Peers" or "Kings) requires an enemy to remain in power.
- Laws are made to prevent actions, not encourage innovation. Can you imagine Congress passing a law requiring Thomas Edison to develop the light bulb or Charles Martin Hall to develop an economical method of refining aluminum?
- The "safety net" in one form or another has existed in our society since before the year, 990[12]. The question is not whether or not to have the "safety net". It seems that over 1000 years of history have settled the issue. The question is how to structure the "safety net" to provide maximum opportunity and incentive to those caught in unfortunate circumstances.

The way to evaluate political proposals is to simplify the proposal by eliminating the extraneous dialogue and charting the inputs and outputs. When the proposals are viewed in this simple form, the results are apparent.

In Thomas Paine's day, the enemy (the "Peers" and the "King") were identified and the solution was apparent. The solution was victory on the battlefield. Today, the identification of the "Wannabe Peers" is difficult. The "Wannabe Peers" carefully conceal their identity. The objective and projected results of their agenda are models of deception. Are all of these agendas that seek to limit our freedom devised with malice and forethought? Probably not; some may actually believe that some surrender of your freedom is in the public interest. They may have the purest motive or a desire to become the next "Hitler". Their motive is irrelevant. Their objective will not affect the results. Don't waste time trying to determine a politician's objectives. Evaluate the agenda. **There is no such thing as benevolent slavery.**

An understanding of the nature of government, wealth and economic systems is necessary to identify the "Wannabe Peers" and understand their proposals. So, before the deception is stripped from their agendas a review of these subjects is provided.

CHAPTER TWO

WEALTH

An understanding of the nature of wealth and how wealth is created is required to evaluate the "Wannabe Peers" agenda, so this chapter defines wealth and how changes in the Nation's wealth affect society.

THE NATION'S WEALTH

COMMONSENSE21C.COM

Some important facts about wealth:

- The quantity of wealth that exists in nature is so small that the statement that wealth does not exist in nature is true. If you find wild blackberries, you have to pick them to convert the wild blackberries into "consumable assets"
- Wealth must be created from the raw materials and the opportunity that exists in nature
- Wealth cannot be consumed before it is created. It is surprising how most of the "Wannabe Peers" agenda ignores this basic fact
- Raw material and energy require labor and intellectual activity to be converted to wealth
- An increase in the nation's wealth benefits the whole of society

There are two primary methods for the individual to accumulate wealth. The first method is to create the wealth; the second is to confiscate it from the creator of the wealth. Confiscation requires force or the threat of force causing conflict. The conflict generally destroys a portion of society's wealth and damages or destroys the source of the wealth. Many times, the conflict caused by confiscation eliminates or reduces any advantage gained by the perpetrator. Confiscation falls into two categories. The first is to rob, steal or use fraud to extract the wealth from the creator (or the benefactor of the creator). These methods are prohibited by laws and can lead to sanctions against the perpetrator. The second method is the use of government power to provide an advantage to the perpetrator's interest or even confiscate and transfer the wealth. In the first case, the perpetrator is a criminal. In the second case the perpetrator is a "Wannabe Peer". Is there any real difference? Of course, persecution of the creator (producer) and confiscation of the wealth inhibits the creation of wealth (innovation). Much of the "Wannabe Peers" plan to increase their power is based upon obtaining control of wealth and the ability to destroy and inhibit the creation of wealth. The destruction or inhibition of the creation of wealth increases poverty, thus increasing the "Wannabe Peers" constituency.

A nation's wealth is the sum of the value of the assets, goods and available services. Wealth must be created before it can be consumed and the most important ingredients in the creation of wealth are freedom, political stability, intelligence, and knowledge. The creation of wealth also requires raw material and energy. Of course, one of the functions of intelligence is to provide the raw material and energy. Unlike energy, wealth can be both created and destroyed. Wealth is consumed and most forms of wealth will eventually become obsolete and worthless due to successful innovation. Because of consumption, destruction and obsolescence, a nation's wealth is constantly being depleted; therefore, the constant replenishment of wealth is a necessity. Wealth takes many forms and may be classified as "Potential Assets", "Active Assets" and "Consumable Assets". Potential Assets (Natural Resources or new technology) require the expenditure of capital to convert them into "Active Assets" (Reserves) before they can be used to produce "Consumable Assets". Production of "Consumable Assets" is necessary to sustain and enhance life.

POTENTIAL ASSETS:
- **Natural Resources:** natural resources are Deposits (minerals, oil, and coal) which are believed to exist. Natural resources require capital investment to prove their existence and prepare them for extraction. In the case of oil, a hole must be drilled and pumping equipment installed. As the capital investment is

made, the asset becomes more valuable. Once the capital investment is successfully completed, the resources become reserves increasing the nation's wealth and providing the raw material and energy used to produce "consumable assets". If the capital investment fails to produce reserves, the capital investment is lost, reducing the nation's wealth. An excellent example would be drilling for oil and getting a "dry hole".

- **Ideas, unproven and undeveloped:** Ideas are man's greatest source of wealth. Yet, an idea unproven, undeveloped and without a market is virtually worthless. The light bulb, the telephone and the computer were once just ideas. When these ideas were developed by an entrepreneur, great wealth was produced. Natural resources, capital investment, labor and human intelligence are required to convert new ideas into wealth. Most successful inventions were once the subject of jokes and ridicule but the inventions that have succeeded in the market place were sources of great wealth. For every idea that produces great wealth, thousands flounder and the cost of those failures reduces the nation's wealth. To be successful, an idea must be sponsored by an inventor and entrepreneur (often the same person) willing to devote his fortune and total being to the success of the project. What is an idea worth? Often, the value of an idea depends on the salesmanship of its sponsor. Many ideas flounder around for years until they find an entrepreneur to champion them. How does society select an idea for development? That depends on who controls the economy. If a "King" or "Peers" make the decision, it is based upon political expediency and often maintaining the "Status Quo". A "Commons'" decision is based upon profit potential. Which do you think is more likely to lead to innovation and the creation of wealth?
- **Land, unused:** There are millions of acres of land in the United States that are undeveloped. Even though it is undeveloped, it has some market value and contributes to the nation's wealth. Much of this land is rich in natural resources. Tremendous wealth can be created by the development of these resources. Regulations that prevent the exploitation of these resources destroy their value and reduce the nation's wealth.

- **Human resources:** we are all "standing on the shoulders" of our forebears. Until we absorb the knowledge developed over the ages, we cannot hope to extend that knowledge. The most effective investment a government can make is the education of its citizens. At the end of World War II, the "GI BILL" was implemented to reward returning veterans for their service to the country[7]. The "GI BILL"[8] gave thousands of veterans an opportunity for a college education. Their education enhanced their productivity and led to unprecedented prosperity in post war America. The education significantly increased the ability of the veterans to produce wealth and the whole nation benefited. The wealth created by the "GI BILL" greatly exceeded the cost and the benefits of that program continue today.

- **ACTIVE ASSETS**: "Active Assets" are production facilities that have been built or developed and are producing consumable wealth. Examples of active assets are:

- **"Reserves":** Reserves are contained in oil wells and mines. The contents of these reserves will be depleted and will have to be replaced. Failure to replace these reserves will result in the reduction of the nation's wealth. However, the reserves may be replaced by other forms of wealth. Technological advances can increase or reduce the demand (and thus the value) of reserves. Natural resources with the lowest capital requirements and extraction costs are depleted first. Over time, the difficulty of converting "resources" to "reserves" increases and the extraction difficulty of the reserves increase. However, the conversion and extraction costs do not necessarily increase. Fortunately, innovation tends to balance the increasing difficulty of harvesting the resources. Since the beginning of the "Industrial Revolution", technology has always increased efficiency and provided new sources of wealth to compensate for the depletion of the more easily available resources. Our nation's wealth continues to increase despite the depletion of the more easily harvested natural resources. Technology, aided by a mostly capitalistic economic system, guarantees us of an expanding economy and improved standard of living but only if we protect our system from the "Wannabe Peers".

- **<u>Manufacturing facilities:</u>** Manufacturing facilities are the tool used to create the "Consumable Assets" and are defined as "active assets". The value of manufacturing facilities is not depleted like the contents of mines and oil wells, but manufacturing facilities do wear out and become obsolete. Eventually, the equipment will become obsolete or wear out. The need for the product's function may be eliminated through innovation, or its products may simply go out of fashion. The manufacturing plant, once a very valuable asset, eventually will become a liability, a casualty of technological progress. To maintain and enhance the nation's wealth, the creation of new manufacturing facilities, making new products is necessary.

- **<u>Infrastructure:</u>** The structures and facilities required to operate our civilization. The value of the capital investment in infrastructure almost defies imagination. Infrastructure is the facilities required for civilization to function. Much of the infrastructure is owned and maintained by the government. The infrastructure provides facilities for transportation of goods, distribution of power, water and disposition of sewerage. When infrastructure is created, it becomes part of the country's wealth. Often, a relatively small investment in the infrastructure can cause a tremendous increase in the value of other assets. An example is the ERIE CANAL[2]. The ERIE CANAL opened up an entire section of the country for commerce. The increase in the value of the land served by the canal exceeded the cost of the canal by a factor of hundreds. The reduction of transportation costs added value to the products, making it economical to produce agricultural products in the area served by the canal. The ERIE CANAL was a large part of the capital investment required to convert the "Potential Asset" (unused land) into an "Active Asset". The cost of the ERIE CANAL was insignificant compared to the increase in the nation's wealth. Unfortunately, not all investments in infrastructure are as successful as the ERIE CANAL. For each "home run" like the ERIE CANAL there are many that simply consume the wealth. An example is a "Wannabe Peers" project to invest in useless infrastructure such as the famed "bridge to nowhere" once planned for Alaska. Since the government owns and operates most of the infrastructure, many of the decisions on what and where to create infrastructure are made by "Wannabe Peers". Of course, the "Wannabe Peers" will make the decision based upon political expediency, not on profit potential that increases the "Nation's Wealth". The creation and maintenance of infrastructure is vital to the economy, but it probably has more potential for the misallocation of capital than any other form of investment in our society. Since wealth is finite, wealth wasted on government boondoggles prevents the creation of worthwhile projects. Misallocation of wealth is destruction of wealth that enhances the long term objective of the "Wannabe Peers".

• **Transportation companies, Wholesale & Retail Facilities, Builders, Service providers, Professional and other businesses which have value:** Often "consumable assets" cannot be consumed at the location where they are produced. Transporting the "consumable assets" to the location where there is demand adds value to the "consumable asset". The ERIE CANAL provided a low cost method of transporting the products produced in the area it served. Before the ERIE CANAL was built, the cost of moving products to market from the area the canal served was prohibitive. The availability of low cost transportation greatly enhanced the value of the products and created tremendous wealth.

• **Consumable Assets:**
The third class of wealth is "consumable assets". As the name implies, "consumable assets" are items whose production has been completed and are ready for consumption. "Consumable assets" include the manufacturers', the wholesalers' and the retailers' inventory, as well as privately owned inventory.

The "systems analysis" of the national wealth is shown in Figure (3). The Nation's Wealth is the total market value of Potential Assets, Active Assets and Consumable Assets. The market value of an asset is the price that the asset would sell for on the open market, not its cost or its "book" value. The "nation's wealth" is the basis for the value of our money. The chart, Figure (3), summarizes the activities that create and deplete wealth. An understanding of this chart is necessary to understand the real effect of the "Wannabe Peers" agenda. The value of the dollar rises and falls with the total value of the "nation's wealth" and the

24

amount of credit and money in circulation. Changes in the value of the dollar may occur rapidly or may take years to fully reflect the changes in national wealth and the amount of credit and money in circulation.

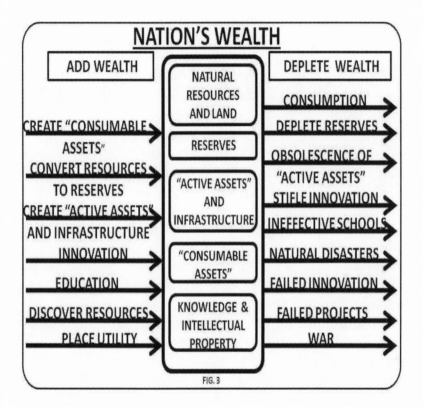

FIG. 3

Wealth and money have a confusing relationship. One of the most valuable rights afforded the individual is the right to exchange one's "best effort" for the "best effort" of others. Barter is one method of accomplishing the exchange, but barter requires two individuals who desire the other's product and that the products are of equal value. If one could simply exchange one's "best effort" for an item of recognized value that could be split into many parts and be used to exchange for many "best efforts" of others, it would simplify the transactions and facilitate commerce. Money, our medium of exchange, was invented to perform this function and to store value.

Originally, money was made of precious metal and the value of the money was the intrinsic value of the metal. Paper money has no intrinsic value. What gives paper money value is the producer's willingness to accept it in payment for the producer's "best effort". It is the producer's "best effort" that gives the money value.

To facilitate the understanding of a system, often the engineer will evaluate that system at the extreme conditions. Applying that technique to the money system, consider a condition where no money or assets exist. The government decides that it wants to distribute bread to the masses and prints dollars to buy the bread. But if there is no bread, the money is worthless. If bread is produced and the producer is willing to exchange the bread for the money, the value of the money is created. At this extreme condition, the value of the dollar is the value of the bread available for purchase with the dollars. If there are no assets available or no one is willing to exchange the assets for money, the money is worthless. This condition existed in the hyper-inflation of 1920's Germany[16].

It is the value of the assets available for purchase that defines the value of money and credit in circulation. Therefore, value of the money is the value of available assets divided by the money and credit in circulation. Please see Figure (4).

Economic changes sometimes occur very slowly. It is possible to inflate the currency without seeing the results immediately. Technological advances reduce the material and labor content of products, constantly reducing the real cost of producing assets and increasing the amount of assets that can be produced with the available labor and material. This "technology dividend" can mask the real inflation rate.

Precious metals were used for money because its supply was limited and it could not be counterfeited. Its value was thought to be secure and inflation proof. An additional advantage was that one could carry a significant amount of wealth on one's person. However, the "Kings" and "Peers" greatly prize the control of the money supply, so ways to compromise the "inflation proof hard currency" were quickly devised. When the Roman Empire started minting coins, the "pieces of silver" were almost pure silver[22]. The pieces of silver contained considerably less than 2 percent silver when the Roman Empire fell. With the acceptance of paper money, control and manipulation of the money supply became even easier. Credit is a form of money and credit is created by the banking system. The creation of credit increases the apparent amount of "money" circulation. Banks are normally allowed to lend up to ten times the value of the sum of their capital and deposits. What this means is that when you deposit one dollar in a savings account, the bank can increase its loan portfolio by nine dollars. Do not despair; history shows that economic expansion (increasing prosperity) generally occurs in periods of slowly expanding money supply.

FIG. 4

Manipulation of the money supply can be used to manage and mismanage the economy. Generally, periods of prosperity occur when the money supply is expanding. Conversely, a recession is usually accompanied by a contraction in the money supply. If the money supply is increased too rapidly, the result is hyperinflation[38]. The producer's confidence in the money is lost and commerce is disrupted. The value of the individual's money is destroyed or considerably reduced, resulting in redistribution of real wealth. Manipulation of the money supply gives the "Kings" and "Wannabe Peers" a powerful tool to advance their agenda, allowing them to obtain control of real assets just by printing money. Inflating the currency is not new. Remember the Roman Emperors, over time, significantly reduced the silver content of their coins[22]. Having to melt, dilute and strike new coins involved much more cost than just printing money.   The power to control the money supply is the power to control the economy and influence the support of the "Pawns".   See Figure (4) for the Systems Analysis of the "VALUE OF THE DOLLAR". The value of the dollar change is not an instantaneous occurrence when the number of dollars in circulation changes. Time is required for the economy to detect and react to the change.   The beneficial effects of the "technology dividend" mitigate the effects of increasing the money supply.

TECHNOLOGY DIVIDEND:

In a free society, the individual strives to reduce the cost and increase the value of the "best effort" that is exchanged for the goods and services produced by others.   Increasing the value of this "best effort" includes both new products, reducing the cost and enhancing the performance of existing products. This innovation continually reduces the cost and increases the quantity of "consumable assets" created per man-hour of labor. It may also provide "consumable assets" with functions previously unavailable at any price (examples are the telephone and light bulb). The net effect of this innovation is to enhance the quality of life and/or reduce the survival effort.

If the quantity of dollars and credit were to remain constant, the cost of goods and services would decline as innovation reduced the cost and enhanced the performance of consumable assets. In practice, the quantity of dollars and credit in circulation increase at a faster rate than innovation can improve productivity.

What is the rate at which the "technology dividend" accrues? One method of defining the "technology dividend" is to use the inflation adjusted "per capita REAL GDP" (Gross Domestic Product). Because of the availability of new products with new functions the GDP probably greatly understates the real value of the "technology dividend". The "per capita REAL GDP" (Gross Domestic Product) [4, 5] adjusted for inflation) has grown at a rate slightly over 2% per year during the last fifty years. Because the growth rate compounds, the actual growth rate was 184% for the last fifty years[5]. Since 1797, the inflation adjusted "per capita REAL GDP" grew 3,217%. The real increase in productivity is probably much greater than the GDP. It is difficult to put a value to the goods and services available today that were not available at any price in the past and the calculations for GDP in the early years is suspect.

PRODUCTION OF "CONSUMABLE ASSETS"

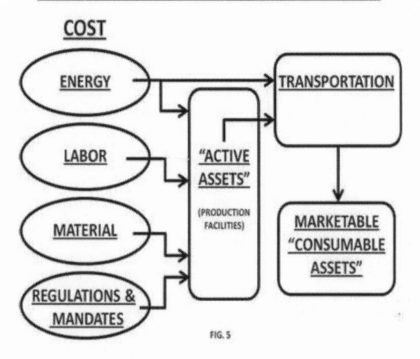

FIG. 5

Even though the use of the GDP to evaluate the "technology dividend" is flawed, it is the best available yard stick. The GDP growth understates the cumulative value of the "technology dividend" but it shows how significant the value of the "technology dividend" is to our society.

Considering the wars, government waste and the effort to maintain the "status quo" during the last fifty years, an average 2%/year is a huge increase in productivity. Without the "technology dividend" the inflation rate over the last fifty years would have been more than double the actual rate.

VALUE OF THE DOLLAR:

While the total assets of the nation determine the value of the dollar in the long run, the total "consumable assets" have a more immediate effect. Figure (5) is a flow chart showing the production of "consumable assets". To understand the "Wannabe Peers" agenda, one must understand Figure 5 and its implications. A favorite tactic of the "Wannabe Peers" is to vilify the producer and propose sanctions to punish the producer. These sanctions always increase the cost of production or reduce the availability of the "consumable assets". These sanctions either increase the "Wannabe Peers'" power or benefit a "Pawn" either as a reward for past support or an inducement to provide support.

The ingredients required to produce "consumable assets" is labor, energy, materials, "active assets", production facilities and transportation. The nation's economy contains limited quantities of these ingredients which limit the capacity to produce "consumable assets". If there is a change in the amount of ingredients required to produce a "consumable asset", the value and availability of that "consumable asset" will change. When innovation (the "Technology Dividend") reduces the amount of ingredients required to produce the "consumable asset", more of the "consumable asset" is available or ingredients are released for other uses. The net effect is that more "consumable assets" become available at a **lower real cost**. All other things being equal, the value of the currency increases as more "consumable assets" become available and the nation becomes more prosperous.

If the quantity or cost of ingredients that is required to produce "consumable assets" increases, the cost of "consumable assets" increases and less "consumable assets" are available. If government regulations are implemented that require an increase in the ingredients in a "consumable asset", less of that product will be available or ingredients will be diverted from other uses. In any event, the cost of the "consumable asset" will increase. The net effect is to reduce the nation's wealth and prosperity suffers. Of course, increasing the cost of "consumable assets" has the greatest effect on the poverty stricken, the very group that the "Wannabe Peers" profess to champion.

All "consumable assets" have energy content. Our industrial society requires tremendous amounts of energy to function. A large increase in the cost of energy will have a catastrophic effect on the economy. Proposals to combat the fairy tale that carbon emissions cause global warming will limit the availability and increase the cost of energy. Energy is one of the prime ingredients of "consumable assets" and in the transportation of those assets to market. Energy availability and cost have a tremendous effect on the nation's wealth. **Your wealth**!

Now that the relationship between wealth and money has been defined, how is wealth created?

Creation of wealth is defined as creating or increasing the value of an asset. Freedom, intellectual activity, labor, energy, education, capital investment, a stable government, transportation, ambition and self preservation are the ingredients in the recipe for the creation of wealth. The cave man had only muscles, intelligence, but minimal knowledge and a desire to survive. His productivity (food from uncultivated plants and hunting small animals) required all of his effort just to survive. But mankind's survival depended on the mind, not physical strength. Intelligence was used to fashion sharp pointed sticks and clubs (innovation and capital investment) to enhance the productivity and provide protection from predators.

Progress was very slow as mankind did not treat the innovator well. Legend has it that <u>Prometheus</u>[8], a character from Greek mythology who stole fire from the gods for man's use, was burned at the stake for his achievement. But mankind retained the fire. Productivity and innovation benefit the whole of society, but it threatens the "Kings" or "Peers" power. Early mankind used the **"Tribal Chief – Witch Doctor"** economic system so the "Kings" or "Peers" enjoyed unlimited use of force against the producer or innovator. The "Kings" used this force to protect their position of authority and confiscate most of the wealth the "Commons" were able to produce. Outstanding productivity, innovation and attempts to protect the fruits of one's labor were downright dangerous. There was little incentive for the "Commons" to increase their productivity as any wealth they produced became the property of the "King" or his partners in crime, the "Peers". Any innovation that attracted attention might be considered proof of witchcraft and result in severe punishment or even death.

Any meaningful creation of wealth would have to wait until the producer – innovator was protected from the "King" and

"Peers". The most important ingredient in the recipe for wealth is "freedom". For thousands of years, innovation was limited to small improvements in the agricultural industry. Wealth is created by the "Commons" but the "Kings" and "Peers" controlled the "throttle" and the "brakes" and during the "Middle Ages" the "Kings", aided by the "Peers", had the "emergency" brake set. The absolute power of the "King" began to erode in the year 1215 (the Magna Carta[21]) but progress was slow. It was not until the late 18TH Century that the "Commons" realized that they were free to innovate and retain some of the wealth. The power of the "King" and "Peers" had been limited but had not been eliminated. That was the start of the "Industrial Revolution[9]". The early "Industrial Revolution" was the development of tools and processes for metal production, etc. The tools improved the efficiency of "muscle" power and the productivity of the worker, thus improving the average citizen's well being. Even with development of tools, productivity was limited by the availability of mechanical energy. Horses on a treadmill, wind and water power (where available) were the only sources to enhance the worker's effort. These sources of mechanical energy were extremely limited and expensive. The only item still missing from the recipe for creation of wealth was the availability of a practical source of mechanical energy. When the "Commons" had freedom, knowledge and capital, it did not take them long to add the final ingredient (Energy) to the recipe. Enter the "Steam Engine[10]". There are descriptions of steam engines dating back to the First Century but practical use for industrial applications was not available until the early 19TH Century. The labor (man-hours) required to produce the basic necessities was significantly reduced.

Freedom, mechanical energy, tools, and education greatly improved the productivity of the "Commons", facilitating the creation of wealth. The productivity of the worker was greatly increased. Of course, the increase in productivity facilitated increases in consumption. But these advantages only occurred in countries where the power of the "Kings" and "Peers" was severely limited or eliminated. In areas where freedom was severely limited, poverty saw no relief.

The improvement in the production of machined parts is an excellent example of how the use of energy and technology enhanced individual productivity. The early lathe operator[23] applied the rotation to the spindle using a foot pedal while applying the cutting tools to the work and measuring the results. Later an apprentice on a bicycle-like device provided the rotational energy to the spindle of the lathe. The mechanical energy required to cut the metal was limited to a portion of the operator's effort or one boy power after the improvement. Cutting speed and depth of cut was severely limited because the amount of mechanical energy that was available required considerable time to produce even the simplest product. The primary cost of the part produced was the material and labor of the two men. There was little capital investment and the energy cost little because the apprentice had to eat, anyway. Once the steam engine was available for industrial applications the net result was a tenfold increase in the productivity of the machinist. The addition of electric motors to the lathe increased the number of speeds and feeds available to the lathe operator further increased the operator's productivity. Then came cutting tools improvements, form tools, the automatic screw machine and the computer operated machine. The cost of metal parts was reduced and the quality was increased. This made machined parts available for uses that had been cost prohibitive before the mechanical energy became available to the machinist. Can you imagine what a car would cost if all the machined parts were produced on the "boy powered lathe". Each improvement increased the productivity of the machinist. Mass produced applications requiring close tolerances became practical. The wealth of the machinist was enhanced as was the wellbeing of all who used his products. The innovation in the machine tool industry continues today. The labor content of metal parts has been reduced from "man days" to "man seconds" and less.

All the products (agricultural, water, television, computers etc.) you use have significant energy content.

The control of available energy greatly affects the cost of everything you buy and restricting energy availability greatly inhibits the creation of wealth. Control of energy is the control of our economy and the power to destroy it, along with your job. Is it any wonder that the "Wannabe Peers" embrace a fraudulent issue like "Global Warming"[6, 7] that gives them control of energy and power to control your life? Control of energy gives the "Wannabe

Peers" a great opportunity to increase the ranks of the poverty stricken "Pawns".

Transportation is as necessary as energy to the creation of wealth and energy cost is a large part of transportation cost. Economists have a term called "Place Utility". This means that the location of an asset affects its value. An example that illustrates "place utility" follows:

You can't swim and are walking on dock. You slip and fall in the water and there is a life preserver on the dock. The life preserver could save your life, but you can't get to it. A passerby throws you the life preserver and saves your life. The life preserver had the ability to save your life but it was useless until the passerby supplied the "Place Utility".

A less dramatic example of how transportation adds to the wealth of the country would be the "Erie Canal". The "Erie Canal" opened a huge area by providing an economical way to move the wealth produced in that area to market.

Wealth can be destroyed and many forms of wealth will become obsolete. As you know, it is much easier to destroy wealth than to create it. Wealth is destroyed by natural disasters, war, and failed investments. Little can be done about natural disasters except to consider the risk when designing buildings and storing wealth. Unfortunately, nature is capable of generating conditions that exceed our specifications. When natural disasters occur, the government uses its assets to mitigate the consequences.

War is a sure destroyer of wealth and much more prolific than natural disasters. "By Right of Conquest" remained the governing rule between nations, even after the "Commons" obtained ingredients of the recipe to produce wealth and demonstrated the advantages of creating wealth over the confiscation of wealth by use of force.

To maintain and extend their power, the "Kings", "Peers" and "Wannabe Peers" require an enemy... The principle of "By Right of Conquest" and the need for an enemy to motivate the "Pawns" are powerful incentives for the "King" and "Peers" belligerent behavior. The "Kings" and "Peers" always covet the wealth of their neighbors. For thousands of years, the principle of "By Right of Conquest" was used by the "Kings" and "Peers" to steal their neighbor's wealth. It was easy to fabricate some grievance to incite the "Pawns" to support the attack on their neighbor. The "Pawns" could also be promised a share of the booty. The war generally destroyed the victim's ability to produce wealth. The war destroyed much wealth and any wealth seized was soon consumed. This left everyone worse off than when the adventure began but it did not stop the "King" looking for a new victim. The instability caused by war was a major factor preventing the creation of wealth even after the Industrial Revolution began. Countries like England and Switzerland, isolated by natural barriers, fared much better than those with borders difficult to defend.

World War II is an excellent example of the invoking "By Right of Conquest" principle by Russia, Japan, Italy and Germany. The need for an external enemy also was prevalent in Russia, Italy and Germany. Real and imaginary grievances were used to justify attacking their neighbor but the real reason was the lust for power and the wealth of the victim. When the principle "By Right of Conquest" is invoked, misjudging your enemy's strength is disastrous and instead of obtaining wealth and power, all four countries were decimated. The infrastructure, production facilities and most consumable assets were destroyed. Russia, being on the winning side fared better, and they evoked the principle, "By Right of Conquest" and confiscated the wealth and seized control of the territory of the vanquished. Russia's action caused years of poverty and misery in Eastern Europe.

The countries that won the war had considerable wealth destroyed. Even though the United States had very little infrastructure damage, five years were spent producing instruments of destruction instead of creating wealth. Instead of innovation pursuing wealth, technology was used to develop new methods of destruction.

After World War II, The United States did not invoke the principle "By Right of Conquest". The United States understood the simple truth of "**THE MORE WE PRODUCE, THE BETTER WE LIVE**". Everyone wins when wealth is produced rather than confiscated. The United States rebuilt its enemies. Both West Germany and Japan soon became economic powerhouses and we all benefited.

To the United States, a war is simply a danger and a drain on the economy. Unless war is necessary to maintain our freedom and way of life, it should be avoided. There is no chance of increasing the nation's wealth by use of force. Wars and threats of war (cold war) had a very negative effect on the United States economy during the Twentieth Century. Initiating the use of force destroys wealth. It does not create wealth.

The foreign "Kings" and "Peers" still lust for power. The need for an external enemy and wealth (which is always depleted by a Totalitarian society) causes conflict with their neighbors. The supporters of the foreign "Kings" and "Peers" vilify the United States because:

- The United States provides proof to their subjects that freedom produces prosperity.

- The United States is an obstacle preventing many of the "Kings" and "Peers" from initiating the use of force against their neighbors.

- All "Kings" and "Peers" stand ready to invoke the principle of "By Right of Conquest". It is not enough to create wealth. Both wealth and freedom require a constant defense.

Innovation causes obsolescence of wealth. Often the innovation is not simply an improvement in the design but a whole new technology. Once, the vacuum tube was used in all electronic devices. When the transistor (solid state electronics) was invented, the vacuum tube and all the equipment used in its manufacture became obsolete. Other fields, not even related to electronics, like the mechanical calculator, clocks and watches were disrupted. Because of the required maintenance, reliability and efficiency of the vacuum tube, most of the devices which used them also became obsolete and lost most of their value very quickly. It cost less to replace the vacuum tube equipment than to maintain it. Even though considerable wealth was made obsolete by the transistor, the wealth created was far greater. Whole new industries like the computer and "Information Technology" became possible. The value of the obsolete vacuum tube production equipment was insignificant compared to the wealth created by the invention of the transistor (solid state electronics).

However, if the vacuum tube production facilities were a large part of your personal wealth, it could have a very negative effect on you personally. If the owners of vacuum tube technology had successfully lobbied the "Wannabe Peers" to pass laws to prevent the use of silicon, perhaps claiming environmental damage, think of the effect that those restrictions would have had on the nation's wealth and your standard of living... Innovation can have a devastating effect on an individual, while providing great benefits to society. Is it any wonder that innovation always has its enemies? It is easy to see how the "Wannabe Peers" can have a devastating effect on the nation's economy, often with only a few people even knowing anything happened.   Beware the power of the bureaucracy.   Remember, the "Wannabe Peers" are experts at hiding the real reasons and effects of their actions.

Laws seldom promote the creation of wealth. The nature of laws is to prevent actions, not encourage them. Can you imagine Congress passing a law requiring Thomas Edison to develop the light bulb? However, a law to protect the kerosene lamp industry by preventing manufacture of the light bulb is easy to imagine.

Destruction of wealth occurs when it is expended on development of worthless projects and infrastructure which has less value than its cost. Labor and material are limited resources. When labor and material are expended on worthless or losing projects, not only is the wealth expended but it is unavailable for worthy projects. Innovation requires capital. To pursue a project, the innovator must believe that the project will be profitable and either have the capital or convince investors to provide that capital. Of course, there is always the "charlatan" with the silver tongue to seduce the investor and skip town with the proceeds or a failure due to an honest mistake, but this method is probably the most effective at eliminating losing projects. The other extreme occurs when the "Wannabe Peers" use the taxpayer's money on questionable projects (Earmarks) with no thought given to the creation of wealth. The "Wannabe Peers" only objective is to gain power or accumulate unearned wealth.

Innovation increases the nation's wealth without increasing the money supply.   We will call this factor the "Technology Dividend".

The "Technology Dividend" is defined as the increase in individual productivity facilitated by the innovation.

The "Technology Dividend" is like "compound interest" as it compounds itself with each new innovation. If all other variables were held constant, the value of money would increase due to the "Technology Dividend". Without the "Technology Dividend" we would still be plowing the ground with a sharpened stick, working from dawn to dark to provide enough food to survive and maintain the "King" in what passed for luxury before the Industrial Revolution. Productivity has been improved such that it takes a minimal amount of work to produce the necessities of life. Since the beginning of the "Industrial Revolution", even those living in poverty have been blessed with luxuries that King George III could never have imagined. Consider how indoor plumbing, the electric light, the ability to cross the Atlantic Ocean safely in a matter of hours, just to name a few of the inventions have enhanced our lives. The "Technology Dividend" has not applied equally to mankind. Where "Kings" and "Peers" still control the government, poverty and despair are still the rule. The "Technology Dividend" is in direct conflict with the "Wannabe Peers" objective of increasing the portion of population living in poverty. Innovation cannot be directly opposed by the "Wannabe Peers". To oppose innovation, the "Wannabe Peers" must use deception, for if their true objectives were to become known; they would lose their standing of moral superiority and be seen as the villains they are. Wealth is destroyed when the government imposes regulations on the producer. Regulations invariably increase the material content, energy content, investment in "active assets" and/or the labor content of "consumable assets". Depending on the demand, either the price will rise or the "Commons" profit will be reduced. In any event, the available labor and/or material will be reduced and less of the product (or something else) will be available for consumption. The nation's wealth will be reduced. In an extreme case, the "Commons" could be bankrupted and the product no longer available, resulting in the loss of all the jobs in the industry (remember Prohibition). Sounds like a good way for the "Wannabe Peers" to push more "Commons" below the poverty line and increase their constituency.

The relationship between "Commons'" wealth and the "nation's wealth" is often misrepresented by the "Wannabe Peers". The "Wannabe Peers" often imply that there is something sinister about the "Commons" (producer) possessing "excessive" wealth and propose government action to limit the producer's retention and enjoyment of the fruits of his success. Figure 5 shows the relationship between the "nation's wealth" and the "Commons'" wealth.

Wealth (Best Effort) produced by the individual "Common" becomes part of the "nation's wealth". In return, the "Common" receives money, which is exchanged for "consumable assets" (the "best effort" of others), to make investments and to pay taxes (this money goes back into circulation). In return for the taxes, governmental services and use of infrastructure are provided. If the amount of money received exceeds the consumable assets purchased, taxes and contributions, the "Common" will have capital available for investment. The investment might be the purchase of a home, bank deposit, stock purchase or be used to enhance the "Commons'" business venture. Upon investment, the money goes back into circulation. If the "Common" fails to invest the surplus and allows it to stagnate, the amount of money and credit in circulation is decreased, thus increasing the value of the currency. If the investment is successful, its value increases and so does the value of "nation's wealth" and the currency. The "Common" only has two rational choices. The wealth must be either consumed or invested. If there are no unfilled needs or desires as is the case with the most productive "Commons", the choice must be investment. The more ambitious "Commons" will forego consumption to finance pursuit of innovation. Progressive Income taxes directly reduce the capital available for investment.

One has to believe that since the "Common" is only concerned with the future value of the investment and the "Wannabe Peers" are mostly concerned with reelection, that "Common" will choose the most efficient use of the capital. If the extra effort the "Commons" must exert produces only the money to pay taxes, there is little incentive for the "Commons" to expend that extra effort. A progressive income tax reduces the availability of capital both by taxes paid and reducing the incentive of the "Commons" to produce wealth. A tax on productivity should be prohibited by the cruel and unusual punishment clause of the Constitution. A tax on consumption makes a lot more sense.

Innovation depends on the new ideas, effort and dedication of the "Commons" and is financed by the "Commons'" ability to produce or obtain capital. Innovation reduces the labor (increases the productivity of the individual) and/or the material content of "consumable assets". Innovation creates new products with functions previously unavailable or too costly to market.

<u>Over **the long term, society cannot consume more than it produces!**</u>

Enhancing your standard of living requires innovation! Freedom of the "Commons" is the most important ingredient in the recipe for the creation of wealth.

The "Wannabe Peers" will continue to try to destroy or inhibit the production of wealth in their pursuit of power and this means stifling of innovation and preventing the development of natural resources. If the "nation's wealth" and our standard of living is to continue to increase, the freedom of the "Commons" and their access to capital must be protected. It is the productivity (product/man-hour) of the "Commons" that defines the nation's wealth" and limits the consumption of wealth.

THE NATION'S AND THE "COMMON'S" WEALTH

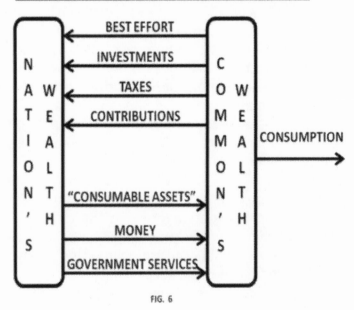

FIG. 6

SUMMARY:
Innovation, discovery and development of natural resources or invoking the principle of "by right of conquest" are the only ways to increase the nation's wealth. The use of "by right of conquest" (force) is a prescription for disaster so the only rational methods of increasing the nation's wealth are to provide the freedom required for innovation, discovery and development of natural resources.

CHAPTER THREE

THE ECONOMIC SYSTEMS

"Wikipedia Encyclopedia" lists 52 different economic systems. Actually, there are only three different classes of economic systems. These are the "Totalitarian", the "Mixed Economy"(cronyism) and "Capitalism". Of the three classes, only "Totalitarian" and "Capitalism" can be rigorously defined. A "Mixed Economy" is as the name implies simply a mixture of the two extremes. The balance of the "Mixed Economy" constantly changes as the "Wannabe Peers" and the "Commons" jockey for advantage. The long term advantage seems to lie with the "Wannabe Peers" as it appears that our freedom erodes with time. Our once near "Capitalist" system is slowly being transformed into a "Totalitarian" economic system.

THE "TOTALITARIAN" SYSTEM:

The "Totalitarian" system is the oldest, most disastrous and oppressive of the economic systems and is marked by instability and poverty.

A simple example of the "Totalitarian" system is the Tribal Chief – Witch Doctor system, the system that has held most of Africa in abject poverty for thousands of years. The Tribal Chief seizes the wealth created by the "Commons". The Witch Doctor then assures the "Commons" that they were privileged to sacrifice to the glory of the Tribal Chief and they will be rewarded for their sacrifice in the "after life". The primary characteristic of the "Totalitarian" system is the use of unlimited physical force by a "King" (sometimes a small committee) to oppress the "Commons". If the political unit becomes too large to be controlled by a single individual, the "King" empowers "Peers" to extend his control. When possible, any achievement by the "Commons" is claimed by the "King" or "Peers". Any achievement which cannot be claimed by the ""King" or "Peers" diminishes their power and prestige.

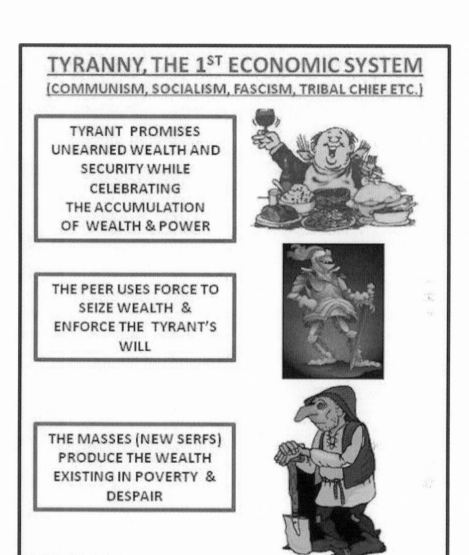

The fear of losing their power and prestige causes the oppression of the "Commons" by the "King" and his "Peers" and prevents the "Commons" from obtaining any meaningful benefit from innovation or their labor. The oppression causes discontent among the "Commons". Measures taken to control the discontent escalates and leads to imprisoning the dissenters and even murder by the "King" or his henchmen, the "Peers". To maintain control of the "Commons", the "King" invents an enemy. The "Commons" are taught to hate or fear this enemy more than the "King". An enemy is necessary for the survival of any "Totalitarian" government. Once the fear of the enemy is established, dissenters can be suppressed by accusing them of collaboration with or giving support to the enemy. This deception disguises the suppression, preventing the other "Commons" from recognizing the injustice.

The "Totalitarian" form of government prevented innovation and progress for thousands of years, but when a "King" achieves control of an industrial society, it can function for years before the economy collapses. Declining productivity caused by economic decisions based upon political expedience and oppression of the "Commons" causes increased dissent. The dissent threatens the "King's" power and further weakens the economy. The thirst for more power and declining ability of the economy to create wealth cause the "King's" relations with the "necessary enemy" to become more aggressive. Eventually, either the conditions become so bad that a revolution replaces the "King" or the "King's" attempts to extract wealth from the "necessary enemy" causes a war. If the war is won, the distribution of some of the confiscated wealth and patriotic fervor gives the "King" wide popularity and allows for the consolidation of power, extending his reign. Losing the war generally results in the "King's" power being destroyed and the "Commons" losing whatever wealth they had been able to hide from the "King". Without the intervention of a benevolent outside force, the fall of the "King" will simply result in a new "King" seizing power. Either way, the cycle starts over. The aggressive behavior of "Totalitarian" governments is the main source of the world's political instability. The fear of attack by a foreign "King" causes free countries to expend considerable wealth for protection.

Do not be fooled, the "Totalitarian" system goes by many names such as Fascism, Socialism, Communism, Kingdom and some that use religious doctrine to justify the blatant use of force against the "Commons" and their neighbors. Call them what you will, there is no real difference. All are characterized by total power exercised by an individual or small group and oppression of the "Commons".
"CAPITALISM":

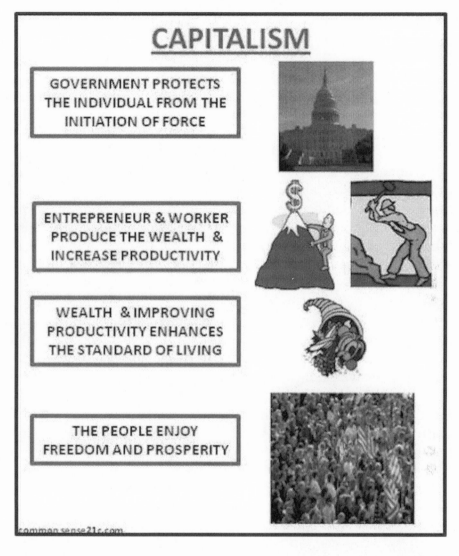

The opposite extreme of a "Totalitarian" system is "Capitalism." Capitalism is an ideal that has never actually existed; it is analogous to "absolute zero" in thermodynamics. Capitalism is simply an economic system based upon maximum individual freedom. If the economic system is based on individual freedom, the government would be limited to protecting the individual from the initiation of force, both foreign and domestic. Because the term "capitalism" is not well understood, the "Wannabe Peers'" agenda will be evaluated by the effect on individual freedom. Pure "Capitalism" may not be practical and might even evolve into a

"Totalitarian" system. However, history indicates that the freer a society is, the more prosperous it is. When The United States won its freedom, the system established was as close to maximum individual freedom (capitalism) as has ever existed. In a free ("Pure Capitalist") society, the government's power would be very limited. Military force to provide protection from foreign "Kings" would certainly be a necessity. A domestic police force would be required to maintain domestic tranquility and protect both the individual and public property from the initiation of force. Government owned or controlled infrastructure would be required to allow the police and army access to provide this protection. A court system would be required to enforce contracts, maintain a record of property ownership, and settle disputes and correct injustices caused by a citizen initiating the use of force against another citizen. Fraud, of course, is a form of force as is any action contaminating private or common property such as the atmosphere, public lakes and streams. The government would be responsible for the management of public property. Unclaimed lands, streams, lakes, beaches, infrastructure required for civil and National Defense are examples of this property.

Taxes would have to be levied to pay for these services and taxes are an infringement on freedom (but not a grievous infringement if levied equally and used to pay for services, **not to control behavior**. Wherever possible, taxes should be linked to the services provided. In a free society, many of the government services could be paid for with the "Technology Dividend" by inflating currency at the rate that productivity improves. Properties owned by the government would be maintained or disposed of for the equal benefit of all citizens.

There are some other less obvious government activities that could be justified because they enhance the general welfare and support the government's obligation to provide for the common defense and maintain domestic tranquility. A very strict interpretation of capitalistic principles might rule out government involvement in such activities as education or the "safety net". Such an interpretation would ignore some important facts. For instance, one could argue that government involvement in education is required in a Capitalistic society because an educated citizen is required for the nation's defense in a highly technological world. Education is one example of government responsibility that is not

46

obvious from the strict definition of individual freedom ("Pure Capitalism"). Encouragement of the individual's education does not mean that the government should operate the school system.

The so called "safety net"[12] for the "unfortunate" might also be justified by the government's responsibility to protect the individual from crime. An individual without food or shelter is in a desperate situation. Without an alternative, the individual will probably resort to violence to survive. Even if you have no compassion for the "unfortunate", a case could be made that it is more economical (and humane) to provide minimum subsistence and aid for rehabilitation to the unfortunate than deal with the crime that such desperation causes.

A philosophical justification of the "safety net" appears to be irrelevant. In our society, forms of the "safety net"[12] were in existence as early as the Tenth Century; our citizens just don't want to see people dying from malnutrition and exposure in the streets. The "safety net" should be structured to offer the maximum opportunity and incentive for the unfortunates to rejoin the productive society, not enhance the budget of the bureaucracy.

Some may consider the reasoning that justifies the "safety net" and "public education" in a free society somewhat of a reach. At worst, these initiatives (properly implemented) would have little effect on freedom and properly implemented, could greatly enhance the general welfare and even produce a profit. The initiatives of education and the "safety net" may well be necessary to maintain our freedom, but the current implementation of these programs certainly fails to do the job.

MIXED ECONOMY – THE CRONYISM ECONOMIC SYSTEM:

In 21ST Century America, we live in a "mixed society"(Cronyism economic system). A good definition of the "mixed society" is the graph shown in Figure (7). The graph is a plot of prosperity vs. freedom. The "Totalitarian society" is shown zero and the "capitalism" is at the maximum extreme on the freedom scale. A "mixed society" is any space between these two extremes.

Historical evidence indicates prosperity increases with freedom. Claiming to support the general welfare, the government of a "mixed society" will use the "Wannabe Peers" version of "benevolent coercion" (the use of force, real or implied) to control reluctant individuals. This action differentiates it from the "capitalistic" ideal. Seldom does the use of force against an individual accomplish long term desirable results. Education and logical persuasion are much more effective in creating real and lasting change. "Benevolent coercion", a charitable term for tyranny, rarely produces desirable long term results and should be avoided except in emergencies (danger from foreign powers).

Both the shape and values shown in Figure 7 are subjective and based upon the author's understanding of history. The graph shows prosperity reaching a maximum very close to pure "Capitalism". History actually shows only that prosperity increases with individual freedom.

There is no historical evidence available for the area of the graph where the "mixed economy" approaches "pure capitalism." There is no evidence because "pure capitalism" has never existed.

The old saying "power corrupts and absolute power corrupts absolutely"[13] applies to all humanity. Without any restraints, a totally unfettered and very successful individual could use economic power to facilitate a coup, thus obtaining the power of a "King" and reverting back to a "Totalitarian" system.

Someday, society may need safeguards to prevent this type of coup. The danger of losing our freedom through the attrition of the "Wannabe Peers" agenda is much greater than that of a coup by an industrial giant. The task of providing safeguards to prevent such a coup can safely be delegated to future generations.

Individual freedom creates prosperity. But is prosperity desirable? A stupid question, you say. Not so. Listen to the "Wannabe Peers" touting "global warming"[7]. True to the principles of the "preponderance of propaganda", they only promise that their program will end human induced climate change. They don't talk about the consequences of their program or that there is no proof that climate change is caused by human activity. The Don Quixote of literature attacked the windmills,

DON QUIXOTE

believing them to be enemies of mankind. The modern Don Quixote (the "Wannabe Peers") would have us build windmills and engage in other forms of "energy alchemy". Make no mistake about it the "Wannabe Peers'" "energy alchemy" will only increase the cost of your energy. All "consumable assets" contain energy. When available energy is reduced or the cost of energy increases, the capacity to produce "consumable assets" is decreased and the cost of consumable assets that are produced increases. Advocating reduced energy availability and increased energy cost is advocating a reduction in prosperity, by definition. The "Wannabe Peers" are not stupid. They recognize the consequences of their proposal but they carefully hide those consequences. However, many of their supporters may actually believe the propaganda. The advocates of the human induced "global warming" theory are telling us that even continuing energy use at the current levels is "environmental suicide". The truth is that the "Wannabe Peers'" and their "energy alchemy" will end your life as you know it and will have no effect on the climate.

Is prosperity desirable? You decide!   Why would anyone advocate such drastic actions without some proof of validity of the theory and hide the consequences?   Remember, prosperity is not in the best interest of the "Wannabe Peers". They find it much more difficult to expand their power during periods of prosperity. The "Wannabe Peers" know that their constituency is diminished by prosperity and expanded by poverty.

Our priority should be to determine which of the issues that have limited our freedom (many with more negative than positive results) should be rescinded or modified. Remember, all programs have produced some positive results for some group or individual. Don't dwell on the positive results without evaluating the consequences. The "Wannabe Peers" will only tell about the positive results.

Any proposal that violates the principles of individual freedom involves the use of force against the "Commons". These proposals range from taxation structured to control behavior, to confiscation of property, to incarceration for victimless crimes and sanctions for violation of non-objective laws or unclear and destructive regulations. An example is the "income tax code" which has been expanded beyond the capability of any individual to understand and comply with it. When you file your income tax return you can never be sure that there is no error that could result in sanctions.

Evaluation of the proposal is simple. Does the proposal violate our freedom? The test is simple. In a free society, the citizen would be free to engage in any activity that did not infringe on the rights of others.   Does the proposal violate that right? Rarely is the loss of the "Commons'" freedom in the best interest of anyone other than "special interest groups".

Many of the current government activities conflict with individual freedom. Some may enhance the lives of some group but all threaten our liberty. To maximize individual liberty, laws would be simplified and many repealed. There would be no victimless crimes. This means that laws regulating individual behavior, such as those controlling drugs and prostitution, would be limited to regulations that protected the public safety and ensuring that erratic behavior caused by drugs took place only in a controlled environment. Sanctions imposed on the perpetrators of crimes would involve restitution instead of incarceration except when incarceration was required to control violence and ensure restitution.

The preceding paragraphs are not meant to be an exhaustive definition of a "mixed society". The purpose is to give the reader an understanding of our economic system and the principles that can be used to improve it. Perhaps absolute individual freedom is not a practical economic system, or at least it may be unacceptable to a majority of the citizens.

In a "Mixed Economy" with a high degree of individual freedom, innovation would cause continual change as old processes and products become obsolete and are replaced by new and more efficient systems. Even though these innovations cause increased wellbeing in the general population, they will cause despair among those who find once valuable skills obsolete or who own the facilities made obsolete by the innovation. Unfortunately, individual economic reverses caused by innovation may change prosperous "Commons" to "Pawns" or "Wannabe Peers", who try to use the force of the government to protect the "status quo". The argument they use will not condemn progress but will use some fabricated reason, such as environmental damage, loss of jobs or even religious dogma. These deceptive arguments can be very effective especially when no campaign opposes the argument. Accepting those deceptive arguments will stifle the compounding of the "Technology Dividend".

Innovation can be very painful in the short run, to those who stand to lose their livelihood or see their property values diminish as a result of innovation. When the government uses its monopoly on force to prevent innovation, we all lose in the long run.

Prosperity is a major consideration in the choice of the balance of our "Mixed Economy" but we must not forget that enhancing the general welfare is also important. Though, prosperity and the general welfare seem to complement each other.

The balance of the "Mixed Economy" that yields maximum prosperity and general welfare will have to be found by trial and error. It is quite likely that some minor violations of individual freedom could result in enhancing the general welfare.

The general welfare is rarely served by restricting individual freedom. Some of these existing programs may yield positive results (but often temporary) and for a minority at the expense of society as a whole. These programs will be vigorously defended by those who believe they are benefiting. All such programs should be subjected to an "Economic Impact Statement" and those found deficient should be eliminated.

The philosophical defense (by Ayn Rand) of maximum individual freedom ("Pure Capitalism") is that it is in everyone's "long term rational selfish best interest" that everyone is protected from the "initiation of physical force". This, of course, is a one sentence oversimplification of Ayn Rand's philosophy[3], by an engineer, not a philosopher. Ayn Rand[3] believed that the initiation of force against an individual is immoral. The website www.**aynrand.org** or her books, "THE FOUNTAINHEAD" and "ATLAS SHRUGGED" will provide the reader with more information on Ayn Rand's philosophy and writings.

The "Mixed Society" is a mixture of freedom and benevolent coercion by the government. America was never a "Pure Capitalistic" society and some of the coercion was not very benevolent. The Post Office was certainly not a capitalistic enterprise; however, The Founding Fathers felt the Post Office was necessary to ensure communications. Slavery was certainly an exception, as was the treatment of the "Tories" (British sympathizers) after independence was won. The principle of "by right of conquest" was applied to the original inhabitants of America. The initiation of physical force against the Indians was certainly a violation of individual freedom. In the late Eighteenth and early Nineteenth Centuries, "by right of conquest" was still a generally accepted principle and the "Technology Dividend" had not had significant time to accrue. Survival was still a very difficult proposition and many man-hours were required to produce the "Consumable Assets" required to survive. Many contradictions to individual freedom and even human behavior as we understand it today existed in the early United States. We cannot judge the "Commons" too harshly for flexing their muscle. Remember, the "Commons" were emerging from thousands of years of oppression during which the guiding principle was "by right of conquest" and the only way to obtain wealth was the use of force. Is it any wonder that the Colonies were less than hospitable to those perceived to be outsiders?

Before the United States won its independence, there was no such thing as a free society and there was much disagreement as to what a government should be. George Washington is reported to have turned down efforts to declare him "King"[18] several times. Even though no "blueprint" for a free society existed, the "Founding Fathers" were able to establish a society with most individuals free to create and enjoy the wealth they created. The "Technology Dividend" exploded. The "Founding Fathers" created a "Mixed Society" that produced unprecedented wealth, even though that society was a mixture of freedom, benevolent coercion and sometimes initiation of force against the individual. The formation of the government did not resolve the question of what the government should be. It just started the "trial and error" effort to create a better government.   The "Commons", concerned with innovation and creation of wealth, competed with the "Wannabe Peers", whose objective was personal power.

If it is truly in the citizen's best interest, would it not be better to gain compliance through education and logical persuasion than the use of force? Of course, issues like funding the "common defense" require participation of all citizens. All citizens reap the benefits of freedom from the initiation of force, economic and political stability provided by the "common defense".

If there were any doubt as to which economic system produced the better standard of living, it should have been resolved by a tale of two Koreas.

In the early 1950's, the Korean War left the Korean peninsula decimated. At the end of the war, the "Totalitarian" government of North Korea remained in power in contrast to South Korea's mixed economy (mostly capitalistic government). Since that time, South Korea's economy[4] has grown to be rated fourth in Asia and thirteenth in the world. North Korea's economy[4] is now twenty-eight in Asia and eighty-fifth in the world. South Korea's "GDP" (gross domestic product) is almost 37 times the North Korean GDP. Even these figures do not adequately describe the famine and misery existing in North Korea.

All the historic evidence shows that the system which provides the most individual freedom provides its citizens with the highest standard of living and more satisfying life. Yet, the United States continues to adopt the portions of the "Wannabe Peers'" agenda which limit freedom, even though most of the country's problems can be traced to the loss of freedom and restrictions placed on the economy by that agenda. This divergence from "Capitalism" seems to be accelerating. If this trend is not reversed, it will be difficult to recover our freedom. The success of the "Wannabe Peers" agenda continually increases the ranks of those dependent on the government, enlarging the "Wannabe Peers" constituency and making recovery from the trend toward the "Totalitarian" society more difficult to reverse.

The government controls vast wealth. Consider the infrastructure, public lands, military hardware, military bases, the postal system, the public school system, airports, the National Parks, government buildings, the gold stored in Fort Knox and other wealth too numerous to mention. The government is similar to a corporation where each citizen is a stockholder. It is the government's responsibility that each citizen benefits equally from the government's wealth. The "Technology Dividend" has had over two hundred years to compound and the man-hours required to produce the "Consumable Assets" required for survival has been reduced to very low levels. Options available for providing aid to the unfortunate are now available at minimal cost to society. Justification for this aid is presented by the vast wealth controlled by the government and the "Technology Dividend" which are the property of every citizen, even though such aid might conflict with some people's concept of "Pure Capitalism". Properly configured, such aid could enhance the productivity of many of the unfortunate and increase prosperity and the general welfare. The "safety net" could even show a profit.

SUMMARY:

History proves that individual freedom enhances prosperity, while tyranny creates poverty. We live in a "Mixed Economy" that includes both individual freedom and what the "Wannabe Peers" would class as "benevolent coercion". While some minimal "benevolent coercion" might be justified by the "common good", one will usually find that the "Wannabe Peers'" definition of the "common good" involves the "common good" of some pressure group at the expense of society. Any agenda that involves the loss of individual freedom should be subjected to a rigorous "economic impact statement" prior to implementation and periodic reviews at intervals after adoption.

CHAPTER FOUR

THE "WANNABE PEERS", THEIR STRATEGY AND TACTICS

A "Wannabe Peer" is a person or group that believes it has the moral right and duty to use the government's monopoly on force to affect social change or even to use that power for their personal benefit. This belief probably has its roots in the doctrine of "The Divine Right ofKings"[30] which promotes the idea that some of us possess greater intelligence and are morally superior to the masses. Being morally superior and possessing such enhanced intelligence, the "Wannabe Peers" believe that it is both their moral duty and right to control the inferior masses and ensure that the wealth, created by the "Commons", is put to the "best use". The "best use", of course, is that use selected by the "Wannabe Peers", often for their own benefit, but with some crumbs left over for the "Pawns".

The tactics and strategy described in this chapter have been executed by the "Wannabe Peers" since before the turn of the Nineteenth Century. Of course, both the tactics and strategy have been upgraded as conditions changed and they observed the successes of foreign despots. The "Wannabe Peers" of the late Nineteenth and the Twentieth Century were content to slowly increase their power, secure in the knowledge that their superior intellect and moral superiority would prevail. Who could doubt that a more orderly world, free of social injustice, would result from their effort? Of course, as their judgment was substituted for the action of the free market, exactly the opposite occurred, just as any unbiased evaluation of history would predict. As the "Wannabe Peers" executed their plan and their power increased, the validity of Lord Acton's quote **"Power tends to corrupt; absolute power corrupts absolutely"** [13] has been proven.

Who are today's "Wannabe Peers? Not an easy question to answer and the answer is probably irrelevant. After all, what difference does it make if the "Wannabe Peers'" spokesperson is the one lusting after your freedom, a dupe who believes his own propaganda, or merely an actor, with an engaging personality and appearance, hired to sell the "Wannabe Peers'" latest assault on your freedom. It is the agenda that destroys individual freedom, not personality or intention of the "Wannabe Peers". The loss of individual freedom is the important issue, not the slave master's personality or identity. Don't dwell on the personalities; it makes no difference if the real "Wannabe King" is the charismatic politician and point man for the distribution of the "preponderance of propaganda" or an old, ugly billionaire who pays the bills and pulls the strings. It is your freedom that is important, not the identity or the intentions of the usurper. The "Wannabe Peers" can disguise their motives and identity, but they cannot protect their agenda from a careful analysis that strips away the "preponderance of propaganda" and exposes the consequences. The motive or real identity of those who seek power to control the individual is irrelevant. The best of intentions cannot change the results.

In the late 1700's, the new nation and the freedom it provided were almost intoxicating to the Colonists as they became citizens of the first real Republic. The "Wannabe Peers'" message of false security and redistribution of wealth in exchange for freedom found few takers until the late Nineteenth Century. By then, conditions had changed and the "Wannabe Peers" had found their constituency and were ready to begin the campaign to reverse the American Revolution. In the late 19th Century the "Wannabe Peers" were ready to implement the tactics and strategy that could reverse the American Revolution.

Will the "Wannabe Peers" give King George III the last laugh?

Modern history has many instances of the "Wannabe Peers" engineering a coup to replace a flawed capitalistic government with a Dictatorship. Those successful coups all involved the following:

- A common enemy
- Control of the "preponderance of propaganda" - dissemination of lies and half truths with no chance of being discredited
- Economic crises following the systematic erosion of individual freedom resulting in the inevitable increase in poverty
- The use of physical force (real or implied) against dissidents
- Charismatic personality of the future dictator
- Promise to "improve foreign relations"
- Patience

Though a tested and proven blue print for the successful coup (replacement of a flawed capitalist system with a dictator) did not exist at the "Turn of the Century", America's "Wannabe Peers" were able to formulate a workable strategic plan to gain power. That plan has been successfully executed and upgraded for over 100 years. The result has been a slow increase of the "Wannabe Peers" power, eroding your freedom and inhibiting the growth of the "technology dividend".

THE "WANNABE PEERS'" PLAN:

The development and execution of the "Wannabe Peers'" plan will be described in the remainder of this chapter.

A COMMON ENEMY:

A basic necessity for a Totalitarian government or the "Wannabe Peers'" is an enemy. Hitler's enemies were the Jews, Communists and Socialists. Mussolini experimented with several enemies, including the church, before selecting the Communists and Socialists. America's "Wannabe Peers" have declared the enemy to be the "Rich". Even the title of the enemy, the "Rich", is part of the lie that is supported by the "Wannabe Peers" control of the "preponderance of propaganda" and an inept opposition.

There are three classes of the "Rich":

- Mr. Paine's "Commons" (the producers and entrepreneurs)
- The "idle rich" the descendants of the early successful "Commons"
- The political hacks that obtained wealth through government intervention in the economy

The actions of the "Wannabe Peers" clearly show that they target only Mr. Paine's "Commons" (the producer), not all of the "Rich". The "Commons" created and retained considerable wealth but their defining characteristic was productivity, not the wealth they accumulated. Eventually the "Commons'" wealth became the property of their descendants. This transfer of wealth created the "idle rich" (though some of the "Commons" heirs continued to be active producers) who had little to do with the creation of the wealth and simply enjoyed the opulence made available by their forebears. It is this "idle rich" class that is resented (falsely) by the general population and taints the word "Rich" in many people's mind.

The political hacks that accumulated wealth by the use of political favors add even more evil connotations to the word "Rich". The political hack class of the "Rich" is both immoral and a drag on the economy...

Both the "idle rich" and the political hacks are the "Wannabe Peers'" partners. Just as wealthy industrialists were the early supporters and funders of both Hitler and Mussolini, the idle rich and political hacks are the primary source of financial support for the "Wannabe Peers". Of the three classes of the "Rich", only one class is the "Wannabe Peers'" real enemy. That enemy is the innovator, or Mr. Paine's "Commons", the creator of wealth.

Because two classes (inherited wealth and political hacks) of the three classes of the "Rich" are the primary financial support of the "Wannabe Peers", they are excluded from the consequences of being the "Wannabe Peers'" enemy, even though the "preponderance of propaganda" campaigns may include disparaging statements concerning the "idle rich" and the political hacks (sometimes termed "lobbyists" for propaganda purposes). Those opposed to the "Wannabe Peers" agenda are often vilified as lobbyists. These two classes are the partners of the "Wannabe Peers'" and benefit from their policies even though they fit most definitions of the term, "Rich".

Where is the proof? The graduated income tax is not a tax on wealth. It is a tax on productivity. If "Wannabe Peers" really wanted to punish the "Rich" as they imply, the "Wannabe Peers'" income tax would be a "net worth" tax (A tax on the individual's "net worth would target all the rich). Fat chance of that; if the "Wannabe Peers" were to advocate a "net worth" tax their financial support would disappear overnight. The "net worth" tax is just as illogical as an income tax, but depending on the specifics, probably would be less of a drag on the economy.

CONTROL OF "PREPONDERANCE OF PROPAGANDA:" [29]

The "New World Encyclopedia" defines propaganda as "a specific type of message presentation directly aimed at influencing the opinions or behavior of people rather than providing objective information". That is a very good description of the "Wannabe Peers" propaganda initiative.

The "Wannabe Peers" consists of a large group of politicians but to execute an effective "preponderance of propaganda" campaign, they require more than politicians making press releases that define a "problem" and propose a solution. A large collection of public figures, pressure groups (the political hacks), "Pawns" and "Wannabe Peers" is required give the illusion of wide spread public support. The enemy, the rich ("Commons"), will be blamed for creating and profiting from the problem. The solution will usually punish the "Commons" (producer) with regulations that increase the cost of production and increase taxes. Of course the net effect is to increase the cost of the product to the consumer.

Press conferences and public interviews are scheduled to start the propaganda surge. Newspapers and magazines run "think pieces" highlighting the injustice, touting the "Wannabe Peers" solution and the proposed punishment of the "Commons". The "Pawns", dependent on the "Wannabe Peers" support for political favors and celebrities (eager to show their altruistic values) make statements of support for the "Wannabe Peers'" solution. All of the participants present only the positive spin on the issue while gloating over the proposed punishment of the "Commons".

Generally, popular support for the issue is secured before the "Commons" even know they are under attack.

Advancement of the "Wannabe Peers'" agenda requires that they control the "preponderance of the propaganda". To obtain this control, the "Wannabe Peers" have to silence the opposition, otherwise the lies and half truths would be exposed. From the late Nineteenth Century to the present, most of their opposition has been so inept that silencing it was hardly worth the effort.

How can the "Wannabe Peers" silence dissidents? Hitler's "Brown Shirts" and Mussolini's "Black Shirts" used physical violence to control public meetings. As their power increased, the thugs destroyed the opponents' property, sometimes even kidnapping or murdering them.

America's "Wannabe Peers" use methods just as effective as open physical violence and less obvious to the public. Threats of prosecution for violation of non-objective laws, IRS investigations and changes in bureaucratic rules and regulations are effective ways to control dissent by successful "Commons". The "preponderance of propaganda" can be invoked to vilify and discredit the victim to gain compliance without having to proceed to the prosecution stage.

ECONOMIC CRISES FOLLOWING THE SYSTEMATIC EROSION OF INDIVIDUAL FREEDOM AND INCREASE IN POVERTY:

The primary constituency of the "Wannabe Peers" is composed of the "Pawns", the poverty stricken, those dependent upon the government for their job, the elite (those expecting political favors), the idle rich and the political hacks. Increasing prosperity reduces "Wannabe Peers" constituency while declining prosperity enhances their constituency.

The majority of poverty stricken is those with limited education and little or no job skills. Many are dependent on government handouts for survival. Any increase in the cost of living simply increases their misery and makes survival more difficult. It also pushes more marginal workers into poverty.

Increases in the cost of basic commodities such as energy can easily destroy the standard of living of those close to the poverty line, destroy jobs and force the relatively comfortable into poverty. The net result is to increase the portion of the population dependent upon the government for survival and increase the dissatisfaction of many who are still able to provide for themselves. The bureaucracy provides minimal subsistence to the unfortunate and bureaucracy's regulations that provide that substance makes the unfortunate's return to self-sufficiency difficult if not impossible.

Of course, when productivity declines due to government action, the "Commons" can always be blamed. The poverty stricken is the portion of the "Wannabe Peers" constituency that is the easiest to increase. Any government action that limits production, or increase the cost of production, will reduce the creation of the nation's wealth and increase the cost of living. When the nation's wealth is reduced, it is the poor that are most affected. A slowdown in economic activity creates the economic crisis that allows the "Wannabe Peers" to increase control of the economy and diminish individual freedom.

Since energy is a component in all "consumable assets", an increase in the cost or availability of energy is the easiest and most effective way to disrupt the economy.

The "Wannabe Peers" know that increasing their constituency is vital in their quest to increase their power. It is evident from their agenda that the "Wannabe Peers" know that prosperity reduces their constituency and poverty increases it. The proposals and programs that the "Wannabe Peers" have successfully enacted show a clear hostility to prosperity.

History clearly shows that an economic crisis is necessary to seize Totalitarian power in a flawed capitalistic society. The "Wannabe Peers" plan has been successfully implemented for over a century. The series of economic crises and wars of the Twentieth Century have each reduced individual freedom and that freedom has not been recovered when the crisis ended. The economic crisis that will provide the opportunity for the coup to reverse the American Revolution is eminent? Laws and bureaucracies now exist (and have for over 70 years) that gives those in power the ability to control individual dissent. For over a century the basic cost of producing "consumable assets" has been slowly increased by government interference in the economy. As one would expect, the "Wannabe Peers" have benefited by huge increases in their constituency.

The punitive government interference in the economy is:

- Creating specifications for "consumable assets" that increase the costs
- Restrictions on harvesting of natural resources
- Meddling in the relationship between employee and employer
- Creating bureaucracies which enforce their regulations on a "guilty until proven innocent" basis
- Non-objective laws that permit prosecution of the "Commons" to control political dissent and extend the "status quo"
- Intimidation of dissenters with threats of prosecution and new regulations that would destroy their business
- Restrictions on creation of new "active assets" (new production facilities) which significantly increase the cost of innovation
- Inflation of dollar

THE USE OF PHYSICAL FORCE (REAL OR IMPLIED) AGAINST DISSIDENTS:

Both Hitler (Brown Shirts and later the SS) and Mussolini (Black Shirts) used paramilitary goons to control the activities of their political opponents.

America's "Wannabe Peers", so far, have been unable to use actual physical force against political opponents. However, they have been successful in passing "non objective" laws such as the Sherman Antitrust Act that allow prosecution based upon the "motive" or "intent" of the alleged perpetrator. Any successful "Common" (producer) can be prosecuted under this law (and later amendments to it) or the law can be used to interfere and cause costly delays in the implementation of business decisions.

Complicated income tax laws that are difficult to comply with, or even understand, lead to threats of prosecution. Complication, misunderstanding and ignorance of these laws lead to prosecutable offenses.

Bureaucracies (the IRS and the EPA are examples) have been established as investigator, judge, jury and prosecutor with the power to declare the victim guilty until proven innocent and punish the victim with civil fines.

Both the "non-objective" laws and the fine levying bureaucracies offer the "Wannabe Peers" powerful tools to control dissent and use intimidation to force support for their proposals. The more successful the "Commons", the more vulnerable they are to this intimidation.

Have these government powers ever been used by the "Wannabe Peers" to gain political advantage? Absolutely; see the BIBLIOGRAPHY notes 35, 63, 64, 65, 66, 69, 70. By their very nature, these activities are covert and the extent of these offenses is difficult to document. Such activities are usually uncovered long after the death of the principals.

When "Wannabe Peers" and bureaucrats wield the power to prosecute indiscriminately and bureaucrats have the power to levy fines and seize property without due process of the law, exercising your individual freedom becomes a risky endeavor and outright dissent becomes financial suicide. Guilt is irrelevant! Mounting a defense against these powerful bureaucracies can destroy or bankrupt any "Common" or political opponent of the successful "WANNABE PEER". It is not necessary for a "Common" to be found guilty to be destroyed by this system. An innocent verdict following a bankrupting defense offers little satisfaction.

Intimidation does not require violence in the streets. Powerful bureaucracies and prosecutors, controlled by the "Wannabe Peers", can be quite effective in their covert actions.

PROMISE TO IMPROVE FOREIGN RELATIONS:

The "Wannabe Peers" are quick to point out that the United States is held in contempt by the bulk of the world's population and if you look at the media coverage in most countries you will find that their media constantly publishes disparaging articles about the United States. Many of these articles blame the prosperity of the United States for their domestic poverty instead of the tyranny of their government. The United States has been the most desired location for those immigrating to a new country for many years. Why would so many people want to immigrate to a country they despise? Most people would rather be prosperous than be a victim and the more intelligent know that they are the victim of the "Kings" and "Peers" who control their government.

Is sacrificing our freedom and prosperity worth gaining approval of the world's despots? Hardly!

PATIENCE:

Patience is the defining characteristic of the "Wannabe Peers'" plan. We are into the second hundred years of execution of their plan. Both Hitler and Mussolini tried to push their ascension faster than the conditions would allow and were set back and spent time in jail as a result.

Since their initial success, marked by the passage of the Sherman Antitrust Act, government controls over the economy and the individual have slowly increased. The rate of destruction of wealth is expanding every day. The patience and perseverance of the "Wannabe Peers" is pushing us ever closer to the eventual economic crisis that will destroy the last vestiges of capitalism.

A SUMMARY - THE "WANNABE PEERS" STRATEGY:

- Obtain control of the "preponderance of propaganda"
- Create and vilify an enemy
- Establish means to intimidate and control dissenters
- Establish coalition of "Pawns" (pressure groups) from those who consider themselves victims and want restitution and vengeance, those who want to use government force to control other's behavior and those who would use government for personal gain
- Institute policies that increase the "Wannabe Peers" core constituency (those living below the poverty level and dependent on the government for survival)
- Create a series of economic crises that result in incremental loss of individual freedom and eventually resulting in a coup that establishes a "King"

A SUMMARY OF THE "WANNABE PEERS" TACTICS:

- Gain control of mainstream media
- All comments and articles on a subject must be consistent but not identical. All propaganda should reinforce preceding efforts and hold the selected enemy responsible
- Select and vilify the enemy. All "preponderance of propaganda" effort should not only sell the proposal but should reinforce the campaign against the enemy
- Establish non-objective laws to intimidate dissenters
- Create bureaucracies with the power to enforce their rules and regulations on a "guilty until proven innocent" basis (Very effective in silencing dissenters)
- Disarm the citizens (gun control)
- Establish programs with rewards for the "Pawns" to obtain their support to build a coalition of pressure groups

- Create victimless crimes to reward "Pawns" whose agenda is behavior control (victimless crimes destroy wealth and provide a mechanism for intimidating dissenters). Enforcement of victimless crimes destroys wealth and causes disruption of the economy
- Make and implement proposals to provide restitution and exact revenge to reward the self professed victims
- Behavior control legislation outlaws whole industries. Prohibition of alcohol is a good example. (destruction of wealth)
- Labor legislation that sanctions the use of physical force by the employees to control the employer's facility to force agreement in labor contracts. These coerced contracts increase the cost of "consumable assets" and in extreme cases can destroy whole industries
- Force the use of government regulations instead of the judgment of the employer to select and promote employees
- Obtain control of energy. All "consumable assets" have energy content and require transportation. Increasing the cost and reducing the availability of energy reduces the standard of living and has the potential to destroy the economy. (Nothing has more potential to increase the "Wannabe Peers'" core constituency.)
- Implement rules and regulations that limit the use of private property without compensation to the property owner. (Limiting the use of the property destroys wealth)
- Limiting the harvesting of natural resources (inhibits the creation of wealth)
- Earmark legislation (deployment of wealth without regard to return on investment is destruction of wealth)
- Inflation of the currency, a covert tax that increases the real wealth controlled by the government. (redeploys wealth to non productive uses, destroys savings which increases the portion of the population dependent on the government for survival)
- Environmental rules and regulations that destroy wealth and increase the cost of living with no return on the investment. (Enhancement of the quality of life is a return on investment and environmental initiatives that maintain and enhance the quality of life are not a part of the "Wannabe Peers" agenda.

Most environmental issues have little, if any, payback and could never pass an "economic impact statement")

- Taxing the "Commons" on productivity destroys their ability to generate capital for economic expansion (redeploys wealth from the most productive uses and destroys the incentive of the "Commons", a devastating effect on the compounding of the "technology dividend")
- Allow immigration of persons who have no wealth and little or no job skills. (an instant increase in the ranks of the poverty stricken and in the "Wannabe Peers" constituency)
- Use charismatic spokespersons to sell their programs and disguise their true objectives
- Use extreme patience and take only what the "Commons" are willing to give up at any given time, avoid conflicts and evaluations that could expose the real effects of proposals (The only possible conclusion of the slow methodical destruction of individual freedom (capitalism) is the economic crisis that reestablishes the power enjoyed by King George III but under new management)

Even before the turn of the Nineteenth Century, the "Wannabe Peers" had selected an enemy and even applied the first sanctions against that enemy. The counter revolution was well underway and the "Commons" had hardly noticed.

The "Wannabe Peers" have executed a successful assault on our individual freedom for over 100 years. The ultimate coup is very close. Today, the same peril exists for our freedom that existed when the "Minutemen" stood on Lexington Green[25]. Will descendants of the **"Sons OF Liberty"** remember the **"Shot Heard Around The world"** and turn back this insidious assault on individual freedom?

CHAPTER FIVE

THE "WANNABE PEERS" SUCCESSFUL ATTACKS ON OUR FREEDOM

The American Revolution destroyed the "Peers" source of power and prestige and established a new source of power, the ballot box. When the British military evacuated the United States, the Colonists (Tories many of them "Peers") who had been loyal to King George III, left with them. Not only had the "Peers" lost their power; they were physically removed from the United States so Mr. Paine's "Peers" no longer existed as a class of citizens in the United States. The battle was won, but not the war. The "Peers" were replaced by the "Wannabe Peers". The "Wannabe Peers" are politicians seeking to achieve the power and prestige enjoyed by King George's "Peers". The "Wannabe Peers" devised the strategy and tactics to guide their quest to regain the power and prestige that the English "Peers" enjoyed.

It took over 100 years from the adoption of the Constitution for the "Wannabe Peers" to win their first important victory. The passage of the Sherman Antitrust Act and creation of the Interstate Commerce Commission was the beginning of a successful and very patient campaign by the "Wannabe Peers" to obtain the power and prestige King George's "Peers" enjoyed. Will they be successful? Can the "Wannabe Peers" usurp control of the wealth the "Commons" create? Can they regain the power to punish the "Commons" who rebel against their "benevolent coercion"? Is the American Revolution doomed?

The issue is still in doubt. We are Twenty-First Century Minutemen, standing on today's **"Lexington Green"** with the "Wannabe Peers'" army of bureaucrats advancing with threats of rules, regulations and prosecution instead of muskets. If we don't reverse the trend, our freedom will be lost forever!

Beginning in the late Nineteenth Century the "Wannabe Peers'" successes have slowly diminished our freedom and reduced the prosperity that could have been provided by individual freedom.

The "preponderance of propaganda" touts new and recent items of the "Wannabe Peers'" agenda. This misinformation reports glowing results from recent programs and promises that the new programs will produce prosperity **while punishing the "Commons" who actually create prosperity.**

All the publicity and hype have created considerable emotional support for the "Wannabe Peers'" recent and new programs. This emotional response to the "preponderance of propaganda" makes a critical evaluation of these programs very difficult and causes many, caught in the emotion of the moment, to refuse to even listen to any criticism of these programs.

The "Wannabe Peers'" new programs are just extensions of their successful programs that simply try to exploit new approaches to limit individual freedom and gain more control over the wealth that the "Commons" produce. The recent and proposed agenda is built on the foundation of the earlier programs and derives support from the unquestioned acceptance of those programs.

Many of these earlier programs are over 100 years old and considerable historical evidence of the failure and disruptive effect of these programs on the economy is available. An additional advantage to using these historic programs to prove the destructive effect of the loss of individual freedom is that the emotional response that resulted in the adoption of these programs has long sense subsided. The individual is much more receptive to a critical analysis of these historical programs than the new programs touted by the "preponderance of propaganda".

The purpose of analyzing the "Wannabe Peers'" historical programs is to demonstrate how restricting individual freedom destroys prosperity and limits the compounding of the "technology dividend". Once the loss of individual freedom has been shown to limit prosperity and provide servitude and chaos instead of security and unearned wealth, that knowledge can be easily applied to the "Wannabe Peers'" recent and proposed agenda.

Be forewarned, the most dangerous effect of the "Wannabe Peers'" agenda is not the devastating effect on our prosperity. **The most grievous effect is the ability of the "Wannabe Peers" to use the power of the bureaucracy and nonobjective laws to stifle political dissent!**

The programs that will be analyzed and the results exposed were all once the "Wannabe Peers'" "showcase programs" and several are still regarded as "land mark" achievements. Those programs are:

- Sherman Antitrust Act[24]
- Bureaucracies
- Inflation and manipulation of the dollar
- Earmarks
- Income tax

SHERMAN ANTITRUST ACT:

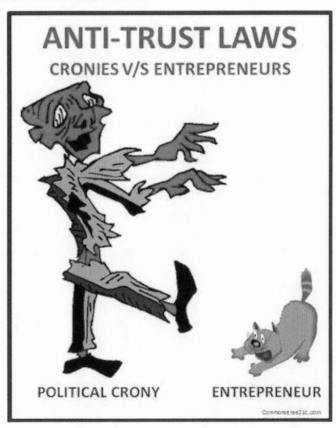

The Sherman Antitrust Act was passed in 1890 and was the first big achievement of the "Wannabe Peers". It passed both the Senate and the House of Representatives with only one dissenting vote. At the time, the Sherman Antitrust Act was not considered an important piece of legislation. Many considered the law too vague to be enforced. How wrong they were; the vagueness was the strength of the law. The Sherman Antitrust Act was a non-objective law. Legality of some actions depended upon the intent or purpose of the "Commons" (producer) so one could never be sure how the courts would rule. The precedents established by years of litigation have made it impossible to operate a large successful business without violating some of those precedents and becoming vulnerable to prosecution.

Of course, this gave the "Wannabe Peers" a powerful tool to control political dissent by any successful "Common". The mere threat of prosecution could cause the "Commons" to support the political agenda of those in power. Even if the "Common" prevailed, the cost of the defense and wasted effort expended would be devastating. The "Wannabe Peers" could offer the "Commons" the option of operating a successful business or engaging in political dissent. Few would choose political dissent with the survival of their business at stake.

The Congressional debate on the Antitrust Law yielded some interesting comments. One of the authors of the Sherman Antitrust Act, Senator George Hoar stated:

"Any company that "got the whole business because nobody could do it as well as he could" would not be in violation of the act. The law attempts to prevent the artificial raising of prices by restriction of trade or supply. In other words, innocent monopoly, or monopoly achieved solely by merit, is perfectly legal, but acts by a monopolist to artificially preserve his status, or nefarious dealings to create a monopoly, are not."

Apparently not all in the Congress agreed with Senator Hoar. During the debate, Representative Mason stated:

"Trusts have made products cheaper, have reduced prices; but if the price of oil, for instance, were reduced to one cent a barrel, it would not right the wrong done to people of this country by the trusts which have destroyed legitimate

competition and driven honest men from legitimate business enterprise."

One would hardly recognize that Congressman Mason was talking about the inefficient producer who was wasting the country's wealth. Some recognized that the Act would harm consumers if it reduced the "Economy of Scale"[42] by breaking up big business and protecting the "status quo".

The Sherman Antitrust Act was sold to the public as protection against monopolistic pricing by the Trusts. It has seldom been used for this purpose. Most complaints have been made by competitors against more efficient companies that were lowering prices to take advantage of the "Economies of Scale". The public was actually benefiting from lower prices but the "technologically challenged" and politically powerful companies were demanding government support to continue their obsolete operations. The public would pay the higher price for the product and the efficient "Commons'" competitive advantage would be neutralized by the legal expenses and effort required for defense.

The "Wannabe Peers" are the only winners. They enhance their political support. The losers are the consumer, the "Commons" and even the "Pawns", who usually only receive a fleeting advantage.

The subject of one of the earliest antitrust prosecution was Standard Oil[33]. That prosecution demonstrated the fallacy of the antitrust laws, even without the political intimidation that the law makes possible.

According to the script, the prosecution of Standard Oil followed the vilification of the company by the early Twentieth Century "muckrakers" [41] in both the press and in books. The primary complaint against Standard Oil was the bankruptcy of their "technologically challenged" competitors.

Standard Oil was one of the earliest and most successful of the Nineteenth Century industrial corporations. It was founded by John D. Rockefeller[43] in 1870 and he ran the company until he retired in 1897. The success of Standard Oil made Mr. Rockefeller the world's richest man. When he died in 1937, Mr. Rockefeller's net worth was estimated at $1.4 billion. Mr. Rockefeller retired from Standard Oil over ten years before the antitrust prosecution of Standard Oil. During Mr. Rockefeller's tenure, Standard Oil developed the technology that created an efficient petroleum industry. That technology reduced the price of kerosene from $0.58 / gallon to $0.0738 /gallon in 15 years and gave Standard Oil almost total control of the petroleum industry. By the time of the prosecution, Standard Oil's technology had been matched by competitors such Associated Oil and Gas, Texaco, Sun Oil and Union Oil and Standard Oil no longer had total control of the industry but it did control the petroleum industry in the Eastern United States.

It is interesting to speculate how an antitrust prosecution that prevented or greatly delayed the development of that technology would have affected the wealth of our nation. That technology significantly reduced the energy cost. The development of the automobile and products using the internal combustion engine would have been economically impossible without the low energy cost made possible by Standard Oil's technology.

To punish Standard Oil for exploiting the consumer by reducing the price on its primary product from $0.58/gallon to $0.0738/gallon and causing competitors who could not meet their prices to go out of business, Standard Oil was prosecuted under the Sherman Antitrust Act.

On May 15, 1911 the US Supreme Court upheld the decision to break up Standard Oil into 34 independent companies with different boards of directors.

If the purpose of prosecuting Standard Oil was to punish Mr. Rockefeller, it failed. Mr. Rockefeller had retired from the company over ten years before the prosecution began in 1909. After the break-up, he still owned 25 percent of the companies that resulted from the break-up. The value of those shares doubled with the break-up and he was already the richest man in the world. In the mid 1990's Mr. Rockefeller's efforts had become mainly philanthropic.

In his essay entitled *Antitrust,* Alan Greenspan made the following evaluation of the long term effects of the Antitrust Laws:

"No one will ever know what new products, processes, machines, and cost-saving mergers failed to come into existence, killed by the Sherman Act before they were born. No one can ever compute the price that all of us have paid for that Act which, by inducing less effective use of capital, has kept

our standard of living lower than would otherwise have been possible."

The use of the government's monopoly on force to protect and perpetuate the inefficient producer can only destroy wealth and retard prosperity. The wealth consumed by the inefficient producer is gone forever and will never be available for economic growth. One of the surest ways to create a "retro-generation" is to use the force of government to protect the inefficient producer.

The damage that the Antitrust Laws have done to the United States economy defies imagination. Despite the technological advances and the "Commons" of the Twentieth Century, the wealth (when evaluated as a percent of the GDP) created by Mr. Rockefeller remains unequalled. We are all the poorer for it and the Antitrust Laws are a large part of the failure of the Twentieth Century "Commons" to equal Mr. Rockefeller's achievement.

The Antitrust Laws give the "Wannabe Peers" a powerful tool to retard and even reverse the growth of the economy, thus increasing the misery and the ranks of their primary constituency, the poor.

BUREAUCRACIES:

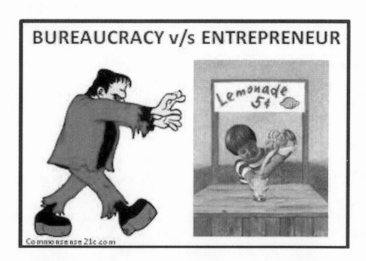

Congress created the fourth branch of government, the bureaucracy, in 1887; when the "Interstate Commerce Commission" (ICC) was established. The ICC was just the first of the bureaucracy that would grow to control much of our life and most of the economic activity. The power of the bureaucracy has grown and many current government agencies exercise the legislative, investigative, prosecutorial, judge and jury function over their area of responsibility. The poor "Commons" snared by the bureaucrat are guilty until proven innocent.

The bureaucracy has the power to;

- Establish regulations without the approval of congress
- Fine the "Commons" who allegedly violate those rules
- Inspect the "Commons'" business without a warrant
- Select the "Commons" to investigate without having to show cause
- Intimidate "Commons" with threats of investigation, fines or rule changes at the suggestion of the "Wannabe Peers"
- Change rules to provide economic advantage to the "Wannabe Peers'" supporters
- Limit political dissent by using the fear of their legislative, prosecutorial and investigative powers.

The establishment of the ICC created these two new terms in political science:

- "Iron Triangle[50]" (see fig. 8) is a description of how the "Special Interest Groups", the Congress (many members are "Wannabe Peers" acting in their own interest) and the bureaucrats act in collusion to exploit the "Commons" and "Pawns". The "Wannabe Peers" objective is to use government force to control the "Commons" and reward the "Pawns" for political support. The bureaucracy is the perfect vehicle to accomplish that. Congress wants to be reelected and increase their individual power and the bureaucracy wants to expand its power and increase its budget. The "Iron Triangle" is the ordinary operation of bureaucracy. It is not unusual for the "Wannabe Peers" and the "Pawns" to trade places as the political advantage shifts. The bureaucrat's only allegiance is to political power.

THE IRON TRIANGLE - THE POLITICS OF COLLUSION

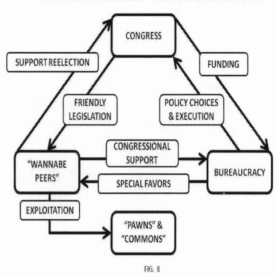

FIG. 8

- "Regulatory Capture"[53] describes the condition that occurs when the bureaucracy matures; the infighting ends and the "Wannabe Peers" achieve control of the regulatory process. They then reap the rewards of the use of government force against competitors and customers ("Commons" or "Pawns"). The "Pawns" (often the consumer) support the creation of the agency in expectation of obtaining favorable treatment from the bureaucrats, ignoring the historical evidence that the "Wannabe Peers" would seize control of the regulatory agency and exploit the "Pawns".

The "Pawns" and "Wannabe Peers" often speak of the evils of the "Regulatory Capture" and the "Iron Triangle". Yet, the evil of the regulations is not determined by who is receiving the "special favors" or who is being exploited. The evil is the fact that it is the agency, not the "free market forces" that controls the economy. When the "free market forces" are perverted we all lose, except those who are the recipient of the "special favors" and many times the recipient enjoys only a fleeting advantage. History is full of "Wannabe Peers" supporting the creation of a bureaucracy and gaining special favors until other "Wannabe Peers" obtain greater political power and reverses the direction of the "special favors", often with disastrous results for those instrumental in the creation of the bureaucracy. Talk about poetic justice.

Bureaucracies are an important part of the "Wannabe Peers'" plan to create the economic crisis that can be used to eradicate the last vestiges of Capitalism (individual freedom). Since the bureaucrats make the rules and regulations, they provide perfect cover for the "Wannabe Peers". If the detrimental effects of the bureaucrats' actions become general knowledge, the "Wannabe Peers" can blame the faceless bureaucrat and promise to correct the problem by "reining in the out of control bureaucracy". Instead of being blamed, the "Wannabe Peers" in Congress spin the problems caused by the bureaucrat's actions to gain political advantage. Many accept the spin and ignore the obvious fact that the bureaucracy was created and controlled by the "Wannabe Peers" in Congress.

By definition, the bureaucratic rules and regulations inhibit or prohibit the creation of wealth. If the bureaucratic rules and regulations were in the best interest of the "Commons", the "technology dividend" compliance would be assured by the forces of the free market and the agency would be irrelevant. The inevitable effect of bureaucratic rules and regulations is to impede economic progress, by maintaining the "status quo", increasing production cost and enforcing a pressure group's agenda. In summary, the bureaucracy is a blatant attack on the "technology dividend" that impedes economic growth and prevents or limits any increase in the standard of living. Continued growth in the bureaucracy can only result in increased poverty. Of course, the net effect of increased poverty will be an increase in the "Wannabe Peers" constituency.

Government agencies exhibit the following characteristics:

- The primary purpose of any bureaucracy is to increase its budget. The bureaucracy's eternal quest is to increase its power to justify an increase in its budget. An increase in the budget means more employees and that means promotions. The increasing of the bureaucrat's budget is equivalent to profit in the "private sector" that allows the company to grow.

- The desire for a larger budget will cause the bureaucracy to attempt to increase its power by expanding the rules and regulations. The bureaucracy power increases come at the expense of individual freedom. The economic damage resulting from this loss of individual freedom compounds with these constant increases in power. The result is growth of the "Wannabe Peers" core constituency, the poor.
- The actions of the bureaucrats, despite the claims to the contrary, are manipulated by the "Wannabe Peers" (the Congress, lobbyists and political appointees).
- The "Wannabe Peers" control the bureaucrat's budget.
- The actions of any government agency are controlled by the "Wannabe Peers" in cooperation with the leaders of the affected industry. Care is always taken to disguise the influence.

Was this fact lost on the "Wannabe Peers" when the first agency was established? Hardly! In 1889, William H. H. Miller[48], US Attorney General, said

"The Commission is, or can be made, of great use to the railroads. It satisfies the popular clamor for a government supervision of the railroads, while at the same time that supervision is almost entirely nominal."

Mr. Miller was describing the first US regulatory agency, the Interstate Commerce Commission. Need more proof that the "Wannabe Peers" knew that the agencies do not act in the public interest? Evaluating the actions of government agencies in 1913, President Woodrow Wilson[52][48] wrote:

"If the government is to tell big business men how to run their business, then don't you see that big business men have to get closer to the government even than they are now? Don't you see that they must capture the government, in order not to be restrained too much by it? Must capture the government? They have already captured it."

These two quotes should erase any doubts that those who were instrumental in afflicting us with these government agencies knew that the agencies were a threat to individual freedom and would try to maintain the "status quo".

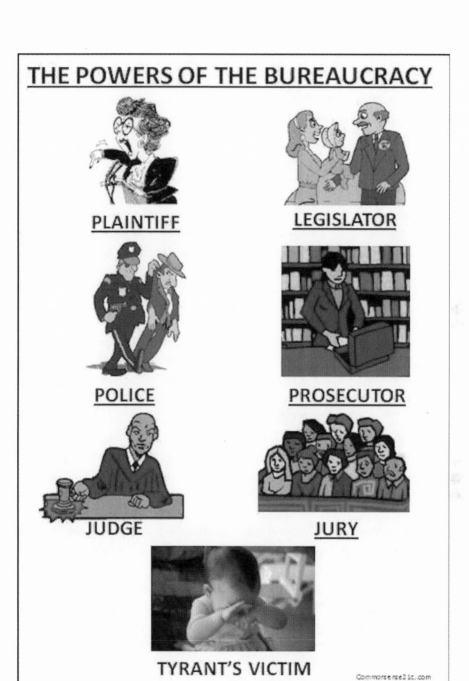

CHAPTER FIVE

The enforcement powers[35, 36, 37] of the bureaucrats provide the "Wannabe Peers" a means of controlling the "Commons", forcing them to support the "Wannabe Peers'" agenda.

A new bureaucracy is created by act of Congress whenever a group of "Wannabe Peers" achieves the influence to cause Congress to act on its behalf. Are the bureaucracies as evil and destructive as this book would have you believe? Reviewing the history of the first of these government agencies, the Interstate Commerce Commission (ICC), created in 1887, provides that proof.

The railroads wanted government enforced cartel which guaranteed them a profit, the Grange and other shippers wanted low and consistent rates and the Congress just wanted to be reelected. Of the three, only the "Wannabe Peers" in Congress were the long term winners.

Within ten years, with the combination of technical expertise and financial resources, the railroads effectively took control of the agency. The "Regulatory Capture" was complete. The railroads had won the battle, but not the war. "Regulatory Capture" made the railroads very profitable for years but "special interest", not even thought of in 1887, would use the ICC against the railroads and destroys the railroad's dominance of the transportation industry. In the late 1800's the railroads, assured of profits and relieved of the necessity of innovation, settled into a period of stagnation. A once proud growing and aggressive industry had been completely neutered by government intervention.

The railroads' dominance of the ICC ended 1906 with the passage of new laws. These laws gave the ICC power to set maximum freight rates and decisions made by the ICC were valid and enforced until they were overturned by a court, effectively making the ICC legislator, judge and jury. A once proud and aggressive industry was effectively neutered. In setting rates, the ICC ended the railroads' practice of granting discounts to volume shippers, thus eliminating the incentive of shippers to cooperate with the railroads to reduce cost and eliminating the "economies of scale".

The United States entered WWI in 1917, and the railroads having lived a somewhat effortless existence under the shelter of the government's benevolent coercion for years, were unable to respond to the requirements of a war time economy. To obtain the transportation required to execute the war effort, the government seized the railroads and operated them until March 1, 1920.

When the railroads were returned to their owners, the regulatory objectives had changed considerably by the "Transportation Act of 1920. The law expanded the rate making powers of the ICC. The Act directed the ICC to set rates to provide a fair return on the entire railroad investment and confiscate earnings exceeding a prescribed rate (labeled "recaptured earnings"). Any incentive for innovation that remained was totally destroyed by the new rules. The railroads entered a new period of stagnation.

The railroads were profitable during the "Roaring Twenties". However, the brief prosperity did not offset the weak credit structures caused by the government operation during the war years and the years of enforced competition (prohibiting the merging of railroads that served the same market) and the ICC's control of freight rates. Preventing the merging required the railroads to maintain duplicate facilities and had made the railroads vulnerable to an economic turndown.

Adding to the problem caused by the weak credit structure was the new competition in the transportation industry. Automobiles, airplanes, water carriers and trucks now competed with the railroads for the transportation dollar. The close regulation of the railroads by the ICC made timely changes to rates and services impossible. The delays caused by waiting for regulatory approval prevented the railroads from being competitive with other forms of transportation. The motor carriers became the new "Wannabe Peers" of the transportation industry and benefited from the "handcuffs" the ICC applied to the railroads. The ICC's manipulation of the transportation industry created the "long haul" trucking industry. Promotion of the "long haul" trucking industry caused huge misapplication of capital and higher overall freight rates. The Teamsters Union became the "Wannabe Peers" and the railroad's status as "Pawns" was absolute.

The financial depression of the 1930's forced many railroads into receivership. Something had to be done to avoid the total collapse of the railroad industry.

Somehow, it never occurred to those in power that the problem could be solved simply by eliminating the ICC and letting the free market produce the solution.

In 1933, the rules to be used in setting rates were changed, requiring the ICC to use more of the analysis that a competent railroad executive would use to set rates. The profit limit (recaptured earnings) was eliminated as was the requirement to create a "National Consolidation Plan".

The other unregulated carriers still enjoyed a significant advantage over the railroads. The "**JOYOUS AND RUDDY**[41]" motor carriers exploited the railroads' regulatory servitude to build an industry (long haul trucking) that could never have existed with an unfettered railroad industry. We all paid higher freight rates and huge investments were made in equipment to create a higher cost, "technologically challenged" industry.

The Congress, having learned nothing from the economic disasters caused by the ICC, passed the Motor Carrier Act of 1935 which made Motor Carriers subject to ICC regulations. In 1940 the Transportation Act of 1940 added the Water Carriers. The political clout of the Motor Carriers and Water Carriers was able to exclude both large and important areas of their business from ICC interference. The Motor Carriers continued to enjoy their status as "Wannabe Peers" in the "Iron Triangle" (see fig. 8).

The Congress passed a "Declaration of National Transportation Policy" declaring that the "Interstate Commerce Act" be administrated so as to preserve the inherent advantages of each mode of transportation. Hey, isn't that what the free market does?

The saga of the ICC had a somewhat happy ending. By the 1970's the regulatory handcuffs had the railroad industry in shambles. Bankruptcies were common and revenue failed to cover the cost of maintenance. Service levels were still deteriorating and rates were rising. Just before the complete collapse of the industry, Congress passed the "Staggers Act" which significantly reduced, but did not completely eliminate the railroad's regulatory burden. However, the Act was adequate to save the railroad industry[56]. Rates, productivity and freight volume had been dormant for over 15 years by 1980. Between 1980 and 2007, productivity of the railroad industry increased by almost a factor of 3[56]. Volume doubled and rates dropped (adjusted for inflation) to half the rates at the time the Staggers Act was passed. The railroad industry, free of some of the regulatory burden, was making a comeback. The Railroad Industry was removed from the endangered species list. Today, railroad freight rates in the United States are the lowest in the world. One wonders what could have been accomplished if the industry were completely deregulated or if the ICC had never existed.

The purpose of evaluating the performance of the ICC is to show how government intervention in the economy destroys prosperity. Evaluating 54 years of the operation of the agency and the rebound of the Railroad Industry, after even partial deregulation, adequately proves the fallacy of the bureaucracy. The point is made but the fiasco of the ICC continued on until 1995 when many of its powers were transferred to other agencies.

Perhaps the progress made by the Railroad Industry since the deregulation is a better measure of bureaucracies' capacity to destroy the economy than analysis of the damage to the economy done by the ICC's regulations.

The ICC did irreparable harm to both the transportation industry and the economy. It is impossible to determine either the cost of this bungling to the economy or the productivity losses due to the stifling of innovation by the regulatory burden.

SUMMARY – BUREAUCRATIC EFFECTS ON THE ECONOMY:

Inequities occur in the free market, but left to its own devices, the free market will correct itself. The bureaucracy will only perpetuate itself.

The analysis of the ICC's performance demonstrated that the purpose of a bureaucracy is to reward the "Wannabe Peers", placate the "Pawns", increase the budget of the bureaucracy and reelect the Congress. The analysis of the performance of the ICC is offered as an example of the normal operation of a bureaucracy. It validates the theories of the "Iron Triangle"[50] and "Regulatory Capture"[53].

Most of the problems in the United States today can be traced to bureaucratic meddling in the economy. The bureaucratic bungling has either created or contributed to the following:
- High cost of health care
- High employment cost

- Dependence on foreign energy
- Deterioration of public education
- Adverse affect on the industrial base
- Extended the life span and the agony of many marginal producers
- Suppressed innovation
- Perpetuated poverty with self serving administration of the welfare effort
- Added to the reelection of many "Wannabe Peers" and their quest for ever increasing power
- Provided a weapon to the "Wannabe Peers" to silence and control opposition to their quest for power

Many man-years of research and reams of paper would be required to detail all the damage that the bureaucracy has done to the economy and individual liberty. Detailing the threats and intimidation to the "Commons" on behalf of the "Wannabe Peers" could consume several lifetimes. This analysis of the ICC's performance and a little imagination provides all the proof of the evils perpetuated by a faceless bureaucracy that any rational person could require.

Is there any doubt that the purpose of the bureaucracy is to increase the power of the "Wannabe Peers"? Correcting the inequities of the free market is not the purpose of the bureaucracy; it is just fodder for the "preponderance of propaganda".

INFLATION AND MANIPULATION OF THE DOLLAR:

A good definition of inflation[62] is "**a general and progressive increase in prices; in inflation everything gets more valuable except money**".

INFLATION - STEALTH TAXATION

THE PRINTING MONEY DOES NOT CREATE WEALTH
THE PRINTING MONEY DILUTES THE VALUE OF THE DOLLAR
PRINTING MONEY IS A TAX ON YOUR BANK ACCOUNT!

commonsense21c.com

Over the long run, the value of the dollar (see fig.4) is equal to the nation's wealth divided by the money/credit supply (number of dollars and available credit). Although many things can cause short term divergence from this formula, eventually the piper must be paid and expanding the money/credit supply will reduce the purchasing power of the dollar. Of course, reducing money/credit supply increases the value of the dollar.

Increasing the cost of real assets also reduces the value of the dollar. The government's meddling in the economy by restricting the availability of "consumable assets", increasing the cost of production, restricting the use of "active assets" (means of production), inhibiting or preventing innovation, increasing the cost of harvesting natural resources and preventing the harvesting of natural resources reduces the value of the dollar. Consumption of assets reduces the value of the dollar as the assets are no longer part of the nation's wealth. When projects or businesses fail to produce value in excess of the investment, the wealth is destroyed instead of being created.

When government regulations cause increased prices to the consumer, those increased prices are blamed on the "Commons" (producer). The "Wannabe Peers'" propaganda campaign against their chosen "enemy", the "Rich", often successfully blames the "Commons" for the results of bureaucratic meddling. Many times the bureaucratic enforced regulations reward the "Wannabe Peers'" supporters {"Pawns") and exploit the "Commons" (producers) while depleting the value of the dollar.

The supply of money and credit is controlled by the Federal Reserve.

Innovation, allowed by individual freedom, increases the nation's wealth and the value of the dollar. Innovation increases individual productivity, the source of the "technology dividend". Bureaucratic regulations and laws, protecting the marginal producer or restricting harvesting of natural resources, increase production cost and deplete the nation's wealth. Bureaucratic rules and laws reducing individual freedom limit innovation. Bureaucracies and legislators can only implement their initiatives by use of force. If their initiatives were in the best interest of the economy (and you), the free market would cause them to be implemented and the use of force would be irrelevant. Therefore, the action of the government is at best neutral and can only reduce the nation's wealth and the value of the dollar.

Taxes remove money and credit from the economy; government expenditures consume assets or invest assets in projects such as infrastructure. The consumed assets are removed from the nation's wealth. The investments, when successful, add to the nation's wealth. When taxes and government expenditures that consume wealth are equal (a rare occurrence) the value of the dollar is unaffected.

THE BIG LIE:

The "Wannabe Peers" would have you believe that tax increases only occur when the legislature enacts or increases a tax. **Not so!** The tax is levied when the government spends the money. Enacting tax only affects how the tax is paid and who pays it. **If taxes don't cover expenditures, inflation results, and everyone who has money pays the tax with the loss of purchasing power.** If money/credit is created to buy the assets, the money/credit supply is increased and the nation's wealth is reduced by consuming the assets. The economy is a complex device and the effect of government spending and tax receipts can take years to be reflected in the value of the dollar. This is especially true when the act is complicated by government borrowing to delay the inflationary effect or significant innovation creates new wealth. With the level of bureaucratic intervention in the economy, the creation of new innovation is highly restricted. Eventually, the loan must be repaid. Since the government rarely has a surplus of tax money over expenses, the only reasonable outcome is increasing the money/credit supply. The government cannot spend money without either using money accumulated by taxes or creating inflation. Inflation is simply "Stealth Taxation".

Manipulation of the medium of exchange, "money", wasn't new to the United States. Over the life of the Roman Empire, the content of the coins[22] changed from almost pure silver to almost pure copper. However, the invention of paper money and bank credit has simplified the manipulation of the money/credit supply for the modern "Wannabe Peers". Even printing money is no longer necessary; the Federal Reserve can expand the money/credit supply with a computer entry.

Control of the money supply by the "Wannabe Peers" requires a government controlled central bank. That requirement was met by the creation of the Federal Reserve which opened for business on November 16, 1914. It opened just in time to use inflating the money/credit supply to finance World War I. The increase in money supply and the production of implements of war instead of "consumable assets" resulted in an inflation rate of 7.64% in 1916 and the inflation rate was above 15% through 1920. Inflating the money supply during the war destroyed much of the value of the dollar and a short depression followed the war. The inflation rate was -10.85% in 1921 and -6.1% in 1922. The manipulation of the money supply to end the inflation created a minor economic crisis. The purpose of the Federal Reserve Board was to end the boom and bust economy that had plagued the country for the past hundred years. It failed in 1920 and the results since 1920 have not been any better. The Federal Reserve could increase the money/credit supply at will but money was backed by gold which placed some limits, at least theoretically. That ended in the mid 1930's when the "Wannabe Peers" succeeded in taking the country off the gold standard.

INFLATION IN THE TWENTIETH CENTURY:

Calculation of the rate of inflation is a complicated and imprecise science. Goods and services that are commonplace today were not available at any price 100 years ago. Innovation creates new or replacement products and services with increased capability so that a simple change in price does not always adequately describe the change in value.

A Google search gives 20 pages of inflation calculators and 4 inflation calculators[55] were used to make the calculations presented in this book.

The inflation rate from 1900 to 2007 was approximately 25. In other words, a $1.00 in 1900 was worth $25.00 in 2007. This inflation rate was mitigated by the growth of the "technology dividend" increased by a factor of 7.7 during that period. The increase of the technology dividend increases the value of the dollar. Without the technology dividend, the inflation rate would have been about 33 times. In other words, without the technology dividend, $1.00 in 1900 would be worth $33.00 in 2007. From 1800 to 1900 the inflation rate was only 1.12. $1.00 in 1800 would have been worth $1.12 in 1900 dollars.

It appears that the rate of inflation is increasing. The inflation rate between 2000 and 2008 was 1.24. $1.00 in 2000 was worth $1.25 in 2008.

Why was there little to no change in the inflation rate during the 1800s yet during the 1900's it was over 25 to 1? Three factors are primarily responsible:

The "Wannabe Peers'" first victories over individual freedom took effect at the turn of the Century (1900). New initiatives by the "Wannabe Peers" added to the earlier victories and the effects compounded throughout the Twentieth Century. Each of these victories increased government control over the individual. Of course, the results of more government control increased the cost of production and limited innovation.

- The nation's wealth was reduced and inflation was the result.
- The creation of the Federal Reserve early in the century simplified the manipulation of the money/credit supply and

gave complete control of the money/credit supply to the "Wannabe Peers".

- In the mid-1930s, the "Wannabe Peers" took the nation off the gold standard. Elimination of the gold standard removed any constraints on the printing of money or creation of credit.

There's no doubt that the rate of inflation increased with the loss of individual freedom and the seizure of the control of the money/credit supply by the "Wannabe Peers".

EFFECTS OF INFLATION:

- Inflation is "**Stealth Taxation**" that gives the "Wannabe Peers" control of goods and services without the "Commons" or "Pawns" even realizing their wealth has been confiscated.
- With a progressive income tax rate, inflation simply increases the effective tax rate without any action from the "Wannabe Peers".
- Replacement of inventory and obsolete or worn out equipment must be made at a higher cost than the original investment, requiring that additional capital be deployed just to stay even.
- Irresponsible expansion of the money/credit supply leads to boom and bust economy, providing the "Wannabe Peers" with a series of economic crises. Each economic crisis provides the "Wannabe Peers" the opportunity to increase their power over the individual.
- Penalizes all creditors. Debt is repaid to creditors with dollars that have lost part of their purchasing power.
- Anticipation of inflation increases the interest rate demanded by creditors.
- Inflation prevents citizens from providing for emergencies and old age, increasing the proportion of the population in poverty, another factor to increase the "Wannabe Peers" constituency.
- Highly regulated industries, exploited by bureaucratic meddling, are prevented from changing prices to compensate for inflation. This prevents the generation of revenue required to maintain and expand services. Eventually the shortfall in revenue creates a crisis allowing the "Wannabe Peers" to blame the "Commons" and usurp more power.
- The inflation rate is not constant. The variation makes it impossible to include the effects in long term planning.

- Inflation makes it difficult, if not impossible, to store value. Storing value is one of the reasons for money.

SUMMARY:

Even an omnipotent President and congressional majority cannot violate the "FIRST LAW OF THERMODYNAMICS". As applied to economics, the "FIRST LAW OF THERMODYNAMICS" means that you can't get something for nothing and that wealth must be created before it can be consumed. Regulations and laws will not create wealth. Regulations and laws can only inhibit creation of wealth or redistribute wealth. Increasing the money/credit supply does not increase the amount of goods and services (the nation's wealth) but it can change who controls the wealth. It allows the "Wannabe Peers" to confiscate the "Commons'" (producer) wealth and redistribute the wealth to the "Pawns" in exchange for political support.

When the "Wannabe Peers" have the power to seize the "Commons" wealth, there is no incentive for the "Commons" to produce wealth!

EARMARKS:

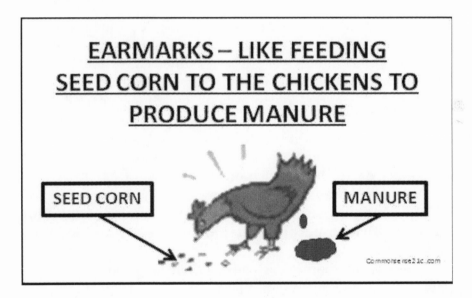

Exactly what is an "Earmark"[54]? Wikipedia, the free encyclopedia[1] lists the following definition of "Earmarks": **"In US politics, an "Earmark" is a congressional provision that directs**

approved funds to be spent on specific projects or that directs specific exemptions from taxes or mandated fees".

A simpler, more direct definition would be **"a law conferring special privileges or distributing wealth to political cronies".** If you accept this definition, unless you were the recipient of the favor why would you ever reelect a Congressperson who sponsored an "Earmark"?

The creation of a new enterprise or project requires capital. If the project is successful, wealth is created. If the project fails, the capital invested in the project is lost. Capitalism requires that the entrepreneur obtain the capital (wealth) to finance a new project. If previous successes have allowed the entrepreneur to create enough wealth, the entrepreneur can finance the project. If the project requires more capital than the entrepreneur possesses, the additional capital must be obtained from investors. To obtain the capital, the entrepreneur must convince investors that the project will create wealth and provide them with a profit. Before they will invest in the project the investors must be convinced both of the personal integrity of the entrepreneur and the validity of the plan that he proposes.

To obtain an "Earmark", the "Wannabe Peer" must convince the Congressperson that providing him with the "Earmark" will be to his political advantage. There is no other consideration. The creation of wealth or profit is not an issue, only political advantage is considered. The real entrepreneur would never request an "Earmark", because to accept money from the government is to accept a partner who is interested in political gain, not creating wealth or profit. The entrepreneur could not compete effectively in the marketplace with such a partner.

Decisions based on political expediency instead of profit potential will only result in the destruction of wealth. **Capitalism is the most efficient method of deploying capital that mankind has yet invented.**

The "Wannabe Peers" use their "preponderance of propaganda" to denounce "Earmarks" **even as they enact new "Earmarks".**

FIG. 9

Even with the best of preparation and maximum effort, many projects fail and the investment and all the effort expended is lost. However, some succeed and produce tremendous wealth. Some examples are Ford Motor Company, Standard Oil, Apple, Google, Microsoft and IBM but the list is endless.

To fund a project with an "Earmark" it is only necessary to convince the Congressperson that it will contribute to reelection.

Have "Earmarks" ever created even a fraction of the wealth produced by a successful private enterprise? Few "Earmarks" expend less wealth than was used to start the Ford Motor Company or Apple Computer or the other private enterprise projects that have produced great wealth. The use of political expediency instead of profit potential to select which projects to fund is a prescription for economic disaster.

Can you imagine an "Earmark" funding Thomas Edison and directing him to develop the light bulb? If an "Earmark" had been passed to fund Thomas Edison's invention of the light bulb, do you think he would have accepted the money along with a partner whose objective was political power instead of profit? Hardly! If he had, we would probably still be using candles or kerosene lamps.

In practice, few "Earmarks" return any value to the Nation's Wealth. Some even return a liability, reducing the Nation's Wealth even more than the original cost. Allowing members of Congress to place an "Earmark" has been used to bribe them to vote for bills they would otherwise oppose. It would be impossible to list all the damage done to our individual freedom and the economy by ""Earmarks"".

In 2008(the latest year that data is available) the appropriations for "Earmarks" totaled $16.5 billion spent on 11,524 "Earmarks". The United States' "Nominal GDP[5]" for 2008 was $14,264.6 billion. So why should we concern ourselves over such a paltry sum of $16.5 billion? After all, it is less than 0.12% of the GDP. The "real GDP per capita[5]" average growth over the last fifty years has been 2.13% per year. This is probably the best available measurement of the increase in individual productivity. So the "Earmarks" consume well over 5% of the yearly growth in productivity.

$16.5 billion could provide the seed money for hundreds of new enterprises with the capacity to create unlimited wealth.

The nation's assets (Energy, labor, active assets (production capacity) and materials) are limited. Once those assets are consumed, they are no longer available for productive use. Most of these assets are used to produce "consumable assets" so the amount of assets available for economic growth is extremely limited. Any waste of this available capital has a significant effect on future economic growth and your prosperity.

More important than the dollar waste are the types of assets squandered. Many of the "Earmarks" are grants for scientific research, paying for the waste of scientific talent and making this talent unavailable for projects that offer real potential for economic growth. The wasteful expenditure of construction materials, labor and equipment limit the useful projects that can be pursued. Other "Earmarks" give political cronies an advantage over their competition, thus raising your cost of living and limiting your opportunities.

Individual freedom (Capitalism) selects projects based upon the belief that the project will produce wealth. "Earmarks" are selected to reward political cronies or create new cronies for support in the next election. The effect of "Earmarks" is to increase the personal power or the personal wealth of the "Wannabe Peers" that propose them.

There are many instances of politicians and others listing questionable or ridiculous "Earmarks". It would serve no purpose to list more of the waste and corruption here. "Earmarks" are more of a threat to individual freedom than the price tag indicates.

THE INCOME TAX:

The income tax was unconstitutional under the original Constitution. The "preponderance of propaganda" convinced the public that the proposed income tax would only apply to the "Rich" and the 16TH Amendment was passed, legalizing the income tax. The Revenue Act of 1913 levied a 1% tax on personal income above $3,000 and a 6% surtax on an income over a half million dollars. Because of inflation, a $3000 income in 1913 is the equivalent of $75,000 in 2008. The original income tax law applied to less than 1% of the population and the "Wannabe Peers" gained political support by punishing their chosen enemy, the "Rich". Changes to the law and inflation soon expanded the income tax base. Soon the public realized that almost everyone was "Rich".

The income tax very quickly became very progressive to finance the First World War. The maximum tax rate was raised to 77% of all income over one million dollars and the minimum rate was lowered to 2% on all income over $2000. In 1952 and 1953, the maximum income tax rate reached a peak of 92% on income over $400,000. Cooler heads prevailed, and by 2003 the peak income tax rate was reduced to 35 percent of the income over $307,050.

A high tax rate (as high as 92%) on a fast-growing business has a devastating effect on the "Commons'" ability to expand their business. The tax made it impossible to internally generate capital required for expansion and very difficult to obtain capital from investors.

The typical "Common" (entrepreneur) works long hours to create the wealth required for expanding the business. Of course, if the government confiscates that wealth it is not available to expand the business.

The progressive income tax is analogous to the farmer feeding his seed corn to the chickens to increase the production of manure. If wealth the "Common" creates is confiscated, the capital required to grow the business must be obtained from other sources. If the entrepreneur accepts capital investment, he loses some of the control of his business. This loss of control affects the ability of the "Common" to make business decisions and sometimes leads to total loss of control of the business. Of course, the threat of confiscation of the wealth by the government reduces the "Commons'" incentive to produce that wealth and increases the difficulty of obtaining capital from investors. That lack of incentive and availability of capital slows or stops the growth of the "technology dividend".

There is considerable risk involved when investing in a new or unproven business. Because of the risk involved, the investor expects to recoup his original investment in less than five years and earn a profit of at least 15% per year. If the business is a corporation and is taxed at a 50% rate, the investor will require a projected profit of over 30 percent in addition to recouping the original investment in less than five years.

Such a profit requirement makes it very difficult to justify an investment in any new and/or unproven business. Only the best of the best could qualify. The "Wannabe Peers" would have you believe that corporate income taxes are paid by corporations. A "for-profit" corporation's only source of revenue is from the sale of its products. Corporate taxes are simply another cost of doing business and must be included in the cost of the company's products. Ultimately the taxes are paid by the corporation's customers. The effect of corporate income taxes and taxes on the entrepreneur simply makes it more difficult to obtain capital for new and unproven businesses and increases the cost of products to the consumer.

Income tax, especially the progressive income tax, is a direct assault on the "technology dividend" and is a big factor in maintaining the "status quo". In addition, it eliminates the "Commons'" (entrepreneur) incentive to create wealth.

The income tax is not a tax on the "Rich." It's a tax on productivity. The very "Rich" simply want to maintain the "status quo" and prevent new technology from destroying the value of their mature business or threatening their dominance in the market place. Remember, it was the very rich "Wannabe Peers" that financed both Hitler's and Mussolini's quest for power. Limiting the "Commons'" (entrepreneur) access to capital has the potential to:

- Prevent new products and services from being offered in the marketplace (benefiting the "Wannabe Peers'" supporters in maintaining the "status quo" and preventing growth in the "technology dividend").
- Force the entrepreneur to yield control of his business to the established competitor.
- Force the "Common" into bankruptcy.

The "Wannabe Peers" routinely change the tax laws to benefit other "Wannabe Peers" and "Pawns" to obtain their political support. These changes continue to complicate the tax code. Between 1955 and 2005 the number of words in the tax code[64] increased by over 425 percent (from 409,000 to 2,139,000 words) and the increase continues today. This increasing complexity of the tax code has caused a corresponding increase in the cost of complying with the tax code as well as the risk of violating it.

The "Tax Foundation's" Special Report[64], "The Rising Cost of Complying with Federal Income Tax", estimates that the cost of complying with The Federal Income Tax Code increased 305 percent between 1990 and 2005 (from $79.7 billion in 1990 to $243.9 billion in 2004). In the same report, the actual cost to the income taxpayer of complying with the income tax code in 2004 was $1.24 for each dollar of revenue collected by the government. Compliance costs on new and small businesses with little or no profit is a cost to the business that greatly exceeds the revenue collected and consumes the businesses' assets that otherwise would be available for growth. Income tax compliance cost on a growing business with little or no profits is a direct assault on the "technology dividend" and it gives the large corporation a huge advantage over the smaller competitor.

The estimate of the cost of income tax compliance in this report does not include the cost for tax planning or tax audit and litigation costs. The cost of operating the Internal Revenue Service is not included. So this estimate is much lower than the actual cost the income tax places on the economy. The complexity of the tax code has continued to increase since 2004 but this report proves the point. Of course, time and effort spent to comply with the tax code and protect one's wealth from the tax man is nonproductive work and that effort is unavailable to expand the business and create wealth. Both the taxes paid and the compliance cost has a devastating effect on the "technology dividend" and the economy.

Considering the high cost of collecting the income tax, can anyone seriously believe that the real purpose of the income tax is to raise revenue for the government?

The purpose of income tax is to allow the "Wannabe Peers" to gain political advantage by appearing to punish their chosen enemy, the "Rich", and to use the power of the IRS to control political dissent and extort political support.

The complexity[64] of the income tax laws makes it almost impossible to determine one's obligation. How do you comply with something you can't even identify? A long enough investigation of almost any business will turn up a failure to comply with some obscure requirement in the tax code. Even if the investigation fails to turn up a violation, the investigation can cost the "Common" (entrepreneur) both wealth and considerable time: wealth and time that "Commons" could use to create wealth. Just the threat of an investigation allows "Wannabe Peers" to control their political opponents or extort political support from "Commons".

The first use of the income tax for purposes other than obtaining government revenue was an attack on the gangsters created by the government's ill fated experiment with Prohibition. When the 18th Amendment to the Constitution was enacted, distribution of alcohol became illegal and the criminal element rushed in to fill the void. The illegal distribution of alcohol was extremely lucrative and the criminal element was able to bribe local government officials, making local prosecution of prohibition offenses very difficult, if not impossible. Criminal gangs in the Chicago area fought for control of alcohol distribution. Gun fights became commonplace on the streets, fueling public outrage. Because of corruption of public officials and witnesses' fear of testifying against the criminals, it was almost impossible to successfully prosecute the well-connected criminals. The Federal

Government used the income tax laws to successfully prosecute these well-connected criminals. Although the conviction on income tax charges resulted in collection of taxes, the primary purpose of the prosecution was to remove a dangerous criminal element from the streets.

The government could hardly be faulted for using whatever tools were available to rid the streets of these criminals. However, it was the first use of the income tax for purposes other than collecting revenue.

The power of the IRS would soon be used for less ethical purposes.

THE "WANNABE PEERS" USE OF THE IRS AGAINST POLITICAL ENEMIES:

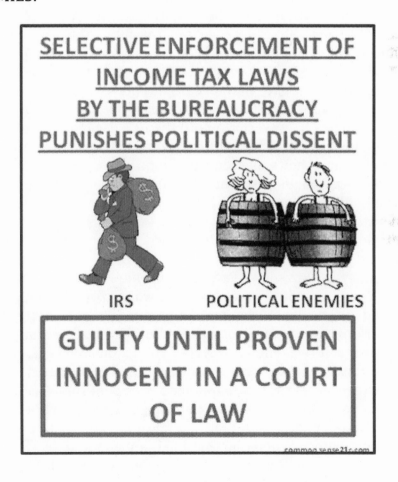

Many of our Presidents have used the power of the Internal Revenue Service against their political opponents.

Herbert Hoover was the first to use the IRS against political enemies. President Hoover ordered the secret FBI investigation[65] of an organization called "Weapons Manufacturers". The investigation was partially based on confidential tax information supplied by the IRS.

Elliott Roosevelt[35] made the following statement about his father, President Roosevelt (FDR), "my father may have been the originator of the concept of employing the IRS as a weapon of political retribution." President Roosevelt's first target using the IRS was Louisiana's Huey Long.

Huey Long was a thorn in the side of President Roosevelt until he was assassinated. Mr. Roosevelt tried various ways to control Mr. Long. None were very successful until he came up with the idea of using the Internal Revenue Service. Mr. Long protested on the floor of the Senate that the IRS sent at least 250 agents into Louisiana to investigate him and his supporters. In 1935, the IRS began prosecuting the more vulnerable (openly corrupt) of Mr. Long's supporters; however, before the IRS was ready to prosecute Mr. Long he was assassinated. Trying to end the prosecutions, Mr. Long's political heirs agreed to support President Roosevelt's reelection campaign in return for having the pending charges dropped. Mr. Long's political machine provided President Roosevelt with 90% of the Louisiana votes in the 1936 election. After the election, the IRS did prosecute a few of the worst offenders; so the first use of the IRS power against political opponents was extremely successful, if somewhat unethical.

There is no doubt that Mr. Long was a corrupt politician and deserved to be prosecuted. However, he was selected for prosecution, not because of the corruption but because of his opposition to President Roosevelt. For instance, Frank Hague, a political boss in Jersey City, was just as corrupt a politician as Mr. Long. However, Mr. Hague supported President Roosevelt, and he received considerable federal patronage for this effort. Even though the IRS had considerable evidence of his corruption, he was never prosecuted. When told that the IRS planned to prosecute Mr. Hague[25], President Roosevelt said **"Forget prosecution. You go tell Frank to knock it off. We can't have this kind of thing going**

on. But keep this quiet. We need Hague's support if we want to win New Jersey."

President Roosevelt (FDR) instigated many IRS investigations against other political enemies. Elliott Roosevelt is quoted as saying **"other men's tax returns continued to fascinate Father in the [nineteen] thirties."** At President Roosevelt's (FDR) direction the IRS investigated William Randolph Hearst, the newspaper publisher, Father Charles Coughlin, host of a religious radio program in Detroit, Boake Carter, another radio commentator, and Hamilton Fish, a Republican congressman from New York State, just to name a few. But in the 1930's, income tax laws were not as complex as they are today and the targets had good accounting practices. Mr. Roosevelt's attempts to use the IRS to silence media personalities were unsuccessful. No evidence of corruption was turned up on Hamilton Fish.

It is not the results of these attempts to use the IRS against political enemies; it is the fact that the attempts were made, that is important. **When government force is used against an individual for political purposes, our freedom is in peril.**

No evidence could be found that President Eisenhower or President Truman used the IRS against their political enemies.

Although the director of the IRS denied that Pres. Kennedy used the IRS against political opponents, there is some evidence that he ordered the IRS to investigate some right wing organizations. David Burnham's statement[65] before the Senate Finance Committee states as follows:

"With the full knowledge of President Kennedy and his brother, the IRS Commissioner of that administration established a program to go after "extremist organizations." Although the memos describing the program said the extremists of concern were on both the right and the left, it appears that all of those who lost their tax exempt status in connection with this program were "fundamentalist conservatives who had been criticizing the President." If true, this was a direct attack on a political opponent using the full force of the federal government. If there were no income tax, "Tax Exempt Status" would have no meaning and this type of intimidation would be impossible.

President Lyndon Johnson[66] tried to control information disseminated by churches, by threatening their tax exempt status.

President Nixon[65] established the "Special Services Staff" "SSS" in the IRS. The purpose of the "SSS" was to use tax records to track "dissident groups and individuals" (President Nixon's political enemies). One of the impeachment counts approved by the "House Judiciary Committee" involved President Nixon's use of the IRS against his political enemies. President Nixon's abuse of the IRS powers may have been even worse than that of FDR.

The more recent abuses have been left to the reader's imagination. No purpose is served by delving into the more recent abuses that may involve the reader's emotions, making an objective evaluation more difficult. These historical examples proved beyond a shadow of a doubt that the "Wannabe Peers" have used the IRS to silence and oppress their political opposition. This practice continues even though the evidence is not included in this book. Most of the evidence of this type of activity (political persecution) does not surface until long after the death of the principals.

SUMMARY:

Income tax makes it more difficult to obtain capital for new businesses and unproven businesses. There's no way to determine the products and technology that have been left undeveloped because of the failure to obtain capital because of income tax.

The effect of the income tax on the "technology dividend" has been considerable, even though there is no way to identify the actual cost to the economy and your standard of living.

Selective investigation and enforcement of the income tax laws by the IRS at the direction the "Wannabe Peers" provide the means to destroy political opposition and is a direct assault on your freedom. It can also be used by the "Wannabe Peers" to reward "Pawns" and obtain political support at your expense.

Lobbying efforts to obtain special exemptions, exceptions and deductions in the income tax laws are a source of political support and campaign funds for the "Wannabe Peers".

The income tax is a perfect fit in the "Wannabe Peers" agenda to regain the power and prestige that "Peers" enjoyed under King George III.

CHAPTER SIX

THE WAY BACK

For over 100 years "Wannabe Peers" have used the preponderance of propaganda to convince the American people that the benevolent coercion (tyranny) of the Government would provide a better life if only they would surrender their freedom for the false promise of security and unearned wealth. The first 5 chapters of this book proved conclusively that individual freedom is the key to prosperity, not tyranny. The fact is that Government coercion can only lead to poverty and injustice. Analysis of 5 of the "Wannabe Peers" "show case" programs, The Sherman Antitrust Act, The Bureaucracy-ICC, Inflation, Earmarks and Income Tax, proves that these programs have led to destruction of wealth. These programs were selected for analysis because each has a long history (some over 100 years). The effects of these programs are well documented in history so the facts cannot be disputed. The advantage of using historical programs is that these programs are free of the emotion incited by the preponderance of propaganda used to expand the "Wannabe Peers" agenda. The "Wannabe Peers", secure in the belief that these 5 programs have general public acceptance, no longer tout these programs with the "preponderance of propaganda". These five programs are historical centerpieces of the "Wannabe Peers" agenda and exhibit all of the fallacies of government coercion. All five programs were shown, conclusively, to destroy individual liberty and wealth. All these programs created poverty instead of prosperity. Both human history and the analysis of these programs prove that freedom creates prosperity while tyranny destroys wealth and increases poverty. This proof means that if a program limits individual freedom, it must also destroy wealth and create poverty. Once you have determined that the program limits individual freedom, that program can be condemned without determining exactly how or why the program destroys wealth and creates poverty. A war or other crisis can make a temporary restriction of individual freedom necessary to protect our country from its enemies but these restrictions should be temporary and end with the crisis.

Do not expect the "Wannabe Peers" to accept this logical analysis of their programs. The preponderance of propaganda routinely ignores and misrepresents facts that do not support the "Wannabe Peers" position. The preponderance of propaganda only publicizes facts that either support the "Wannabe Peers" agenda or spins the meaning of those facts to support their agenda. An unbiased review of the results of these five programs leaves no doubt that each of these programs attacks individual freedom, destroys wealth, increases poverty and limits the growth of the "technology dividend".

Either the "Wannabe Peers" are incredibly naïve or their long-term purpose is to create the economic crisis that will culminate in a Totalitarian government.

The "Wannabe Peers" have enacted many programs that suppress freedom and are proposing many more. Many of these new programs are just as destructive as the five programs analyzed in Chapter 5 and build on the base provided by these five programs. It is tempting to explain the fallacies of these new programs and proposals but it would only complicate the book and put the book in direct conflict with the emotion resulting from the current "preponderance of propaganda". Sufficient proof has been presented to validate the principles and conclusions that freedom creates prosperity and coercion creates poverty. If the reader disagrees with that premise, more argument will be futile. The reader who rejects these basic premises probably stopped reading after the first chapter. The reader, who agrees with the basic premises of this book, does not need any additional proof to reject the "Wannabe Peers" false promises. More specifics on the effects of other programs and current proposals would just be a waste of time.

Four of the five programs, in addition to creating poverty and destroying individual freedom, allow the "Wannabe Peers" to use government force to oppress political enemies and coerce the "Commons" to support their agenda. The "Wannabe Peers" have the power to financially destroy or even jail political opponents and this power will make recovering our freedom very difficult. Unless the "Wannabe Peers" can be stripped of this power to destroy the political opposition, reversing the trend that is destroying your individual freedom will be impossible. If the financial destruction isn't enough; criminal prosecution is available to the IRS in tax evasion cases. Even though the author of this book has been retired for over 10 years and has had almost no income during that period, you can bet that he will be the target of an IRS audit, if this book is successful. If this book is very, very successful, the preponderance of propaganda will attack the writer's character with the expectation that exposing character flaws will somehow invalidate the facts, logic and the conclusions presented in this book.

It took over 100 years to create this mess and an instantaneous solution is not possible. The change must be slow and methodical to avoid the economic crisis that is the "Wannabe Peers" objective. To regain our freedom, we will have to exercise patience just as the "Wannabe Peers" have exercised patience for over 100 years to usurp our freedom.

The use of force and violence would only create the crisis that the "Wannabe Peers" have worked for. That crisis would cause chaos allowing a "Wannabe King" to seize power by restoring order. There will not be another George Washington who refuses the crown. Instead, the "Wannabe King" will promise to "maintain order until stability can be maintained and provide free elections within 18 months". At least that is the promise Castro made to Cuba in the "MANIFESTO OF THE SIERRA MAESTRA[17]". Of course, Cuba is still waiting for those free elections. Widespread armed confrontation between our citizens and the government can only result in the establishment of a Totalitarian government and the "Wannabe Peers" (perhaps not those in control at the start of the conflict) will win by default.

The "preponderance of propaganda" is a master of misdirection as well as misinformation. To regain our freedom, it will be necessary to maintain focus on a narrow set of objectives; do not let the "Wannabe Peers" use emotional issues to move your attention to irrelevant, but emotionally charged issues. The use of issues such as entitlement programs invoke strong emotions with people concerned about loafers consuming unearned wealth and while others are concerned about the survival and suffering of the indigent.

Instances of government provided welfare[12] have been with us since the late Tenth Century. The simple fact is that we simply will not allow our fellow citizens to die of malnutrition and exposure in the streets. Some form of welfare will be with us because of the inherent compassion most people feel toward our fellow citizens. In 1776, it took long hours (forty acres and a mule) to produce the bare necessities of life. Any wealth expended on the indigent was a severe drain on the economy.

The "Wannabe Peers" still point to the long work hours required to produce the wealth for survival in the late Nineteenth and early Twentieth Century as exploitation of the worker. It was not exploitation of the worker that caused the long work hours; it was lower individual productivity. Today, the cost to the economy of providing adequate food and shelter is minimal. Between the years 1900 and 2000 the percent of the workforce employed in agriculture[67] declined from 41 percent to 1.9 percent. Even with that low percentage working in agriculture, 91 percent of the farmers only farm part time. In the year 2000, the portion of the GDP (gross domestic product) produced by agriculture was only 0.7 percent of the total United States' GDP[67]. The average growth per year of the "technology dividend" over the last fifty years was 2.13 percent. Properly administered, the cost to the economy of providing a safety net would not exceed the deflationary effect of the technology dividend. This assumes that we are successful in regaining our freedom and removing the regulatory brakes from the economy. The ambition created by the renewed freedom will leave few people content to accept the bare subsistence offered by a safety net and those trapped there will work to regain a place in productive society. The issue of entitlements will solve itself when freedom is restored.

Along with touting entitlement issues, the preponderance of propaganda will continue to try to play special interest groups against each other and the general population. The "Wannabe Peers" will continue to attack their chosen enemy, the "Rich". Ignore these distractions. Remember, only individuals have rights and any special rights provided to special interests must first be taken from the individual. The "Wannabe Peers" enemy, defined as the "Rich", is not really the rich. The "Wannabe Peers" enemy is the "Commons" (producer) and harassment of the producer is not in the best interest of the consumer.

The important objective is to regain our freedom. If we fail to regain our freedom, we will all be on the government dole but there will be little or nothing for the "Wannabe Peers" to distribute.

The entitlement issue, special rights for special interests and harassment of the "Wannabe Peers" chosen enemy are just distractions and must be ignored. The purpose of the preponderance of propaganda on these issues is simply to induce you to make emotional decisions to surrender more of your freedom.

HOW DO WE GET OUT OF THIS MESS?
THE SOLUTION TO POLITICALLY MOTIVATED PROSECUTION:

As long as the "Wannabe Peers" have the power to financially destroy and/or incarcerate political opponents[35, 63, 64, 65, 66], they will have the power to neutralize any effective opposition. The income tax code and other bureaucratic rules and regulations are all attacks on individual freedom. Yet it is not these programs that are the greatest danger to our freedom. The greatest danger to the Republic is the "Wannabe Peers" use of the IRS and other bureaucracies to investigate, harass and prosecute political enemies. Serious attempts to reverse the assaults on individual freedom or replace the income tax will be suicide while the "Wannabe Peers" retain the power to use the IRS and other bureaucracies to investigate, harass and prosecute dissents. Even without the use of force by the bureaucracy, the "politics of personal destruction" represented by the "Wannabe Peers" control of the preponderance of propaganda is a serious obstacle.

The "Wannabe Peers" use of regulatory agencies and the IRS to control or destroy their political enemies get very little, if any, press coverage. Most of the instances uncovered by the research for this book were documented long after the crime and by then it was old news. Evidence of political persecution is difficult to obtain and usually only surfaces years after the principals have passed into history. Do not discount the danger simply because it is ignored by the puppet media.

Since 1977 most of the information on "Wannabe Peers" political use of the IRS[68] involves investigations of tax exempt organizations' political activities against the "Wannabe Peers" in power. The objective was to silence the dissent by eliminating the favorable tax treatment extended to charitable, non-profit and religious organizations.

There was also some information concerning use of the IRS against personal enemies of the President.

"What do you expect when you sue the President?" Paul Breslan[70], a senior IRS official, told the "Judicial Watch", a Washington-based legal watchdog group that had filed over 50 legal actions against the Clinton administration and was under investigation by the IRS. This audit of "Judicial Watch" was in 1998. Apparently this "senior" IRS official believed that it was the duty of the IRS to audit (prosecute) the President's political enemies. Did you really think the only purpose of the IRS was just to collect taxes? Just the threat of retaliation by the IRS has a chilling effect on potential dissenters.

The extent to which the IRS is used against political enemies of the "Wannabe Peers" in recent history is probably understated in this book. Much of President Roosevelt's (FDR) unethical, if not criminal use of the IRS did not become public until well over 10 years after his death. The threat exists and even if the use is not fully documented for the recent past, that threat must be removed before an effective campaign to regain our freedom can succeed.

Our purpose is to document and prove this grave threat to regaining our freedom, not to judge or demonize past Presidents. The evidence clearly shows that for over 75 years some of our Presidents have used the power of the IRS to retaliate against political opponents and even personal enemies. Generally, the purpose was to control and even eliminate political dissent. While one would hope that a person who achieved the Presidency of the United States would be above such unethical practices, it is not the Presidents that are to blame.

The blame belongs to a system that permits such abuses of government power. We cannot expect "Wannabe Peers" to forego such an opportunity to enhance their personal power when the system offers that opportunity.

The IRS, while perhaps the most widely used bureaucracy to control political dissent, is not the only source of abuse. Any government agency that possesses the power to create rules and regulations and enforce those rules and regulations as investigator, prosecutor, judge and jury can be used for the same purpose. While these bureaucracies have considerable power, it is generally only useful against the more successful "Commons", not the individual. The ability of a bureaucracy to make and enforce rules and regulations without congressional action or oversight by the courts, presents a powerful force to control political dissent by successful "Commons" (producers).

An accused criminal has more protection from malicious prosecution than the political dissenter or the "Commons" (producer) whose only crime is the attempt to create wealth. To prosecute an alleged criminal, an indictment requiring some proof of violation of the law, is required. For the IRS to audit a victim, only a hint from a powerful "Wannabe Peer" is required. Make no mistake about it; an IRS audit is a prosecution except that the IRS acts as both judge and jury. An IRS audit can easily result in criminal prosecution and the whole process can easily cost more than the alleged tax liability even if the victim prevails. If the victim does prevail, nothing prevents the IRS from finding another alleged violation to audit, unlike the criminal who is protected by "double jeopardy".

How on earth did we get ourselves in such a mess? Even more important, how do we regain our freedom?

Of course, abolishing the IRS and all the other bureaucracies would also abolish the abuses of power described above but such an abrupt change in conditions would certainly result in chaos. Besides, such a law would never be passed by the Congress and if it were to pass, the President would certainly veto it. Even though the system has many faults it does maintain order and secures the wealth required to operate the government.

A campaign to restore individual freedom cannot be effective while the "Wannabe Peers" have the ability to use the power of the government to punish and silence political dissent. **ELIMINATION OF THE ABILITY OF THE "WANNABE PEERS" TO USE THE POWER OF THE GOVERNMENT TO PROSECUTE AND DESTROY POLITICAL OPPOSITION HAS TO BE THE FIRST PRIORITY OF ANY EFFORT TO REVERSE THE TREND THAT IS DESTROYING OUR FREEDOM AND PROSPERITY.**

Make no mistake about it; the "Wannabe Peers" will use all their power and the preponderance of propaganda to maintain a system that allows them to use government force to stifle political dissent. The first step to diminish that power will have to be small and so popular that the "Wannabe Peers" will not dare to openly oppose it. Not even the most resourceful "Wannabe Peer" would try to justify selection of the bureaucrats' targets based upon political activity of the victim.

Their arguments will be that any restriction or requirement to justify the selection of the bureaucrat's target will cost too much and reduce the efficiency of the bureaucracy.

The first objective in the agenda to regain our freedom must be to establish a "**Permanent Independent Counsel**," with full prosecutorial and subpoena power to investigate the selection of the bureaucrat's victims. If one claimed to be the victim of a political vendetta, the Independent Counsel would require that the prosecution of the victim be suspended until the Independent Counsel's investigation was complete and had proven beyond a reasonable doubt that valid probable cause for the investigation was possessed by the bureaucrat prior to initiating the prosecution. If the probable cause were invalid the Independent Counsel would have the duty to start both criminal and civil action against the responsible perpetrator (bureaucrat and/or "Wannabe Peer").

To create an Independent Counsel with the power to eliminate the potential for this misuse of power it will require a massive "grass roots" effort. Perhaps this book will inspire a freedom orientated PAC (political action committee) to champion the cause and provide the leadership to remove this source of power (persecution of political enemies) from the "Wannabe Peers" arsenal. If there were ever a cause that transcends party lines, this is it. There is no other issue with both broad emotional and intellectual appeal than political persecution. PACS live on donations and the potential for donations for this cause cannot be underestimated. Perhaps a PAC will see the potential and champion this cause.

When this proposal is introduced, the "Wannabe Peers" will try to amend the proposed law to eliminate its effectiveness while claiming to support the objective. Do not let them fool you; your freedom depends on it! It is not the efficiency of the bureaucracy that is important. Your freedom and above all, justice, is the important objective.

There is nothing that poses a greater threat to the Republic and your freedom than the "Wannabe Peers" ability to prosecute political dissenters! It won't be easy to obtain this first objective but until "Wannabe Peers" power to prosecute political enemies is eliminated; any effort to regain our freedom is doomed to failure.

Once the "Wannabe Peers" power to prosecute political opponents has been ended, the next grave threat to our freedom is the power of the bureaucracy to act as legislator, investigator, prosecutor, judge and jury.

ELIMINATE THE BUREAUCRACY:

The bureaucracy is a fourth branch of the Government created by the Congress to escape the blame for its actions. **The fourth branch of government must be eliminated!** Establishing a powerful Independent Counsel will add protection to the individual from malicious prosecution for political activity but considerable potential still exists for the "Wannabe Peers" to use the bureaucracy to eliminate opposition and extort support from "Commons". If the leaders of industry (particularly new or fast growing industry) are effectively silenced, it threatens the freedom of all and presents a threat to the "technology dividend".

Total elimination of this fourth branch of government is necessary to secure our freedom! Again, we must exercise patience. Although these rules, regulations and the enforcement mechanism have a destructive effect on the economy, stability must be maintained. Sudden removal of the bureaucracy would cause chaos and crisis. The economic crisis that the "Wannabe Peers" have been seeking might well result. Some of those rules and regulations may be necessary and should not be discarded without evaluation. Remember the "iron triangle" described in Chapter 5. Most of these regulations were the result of "Wannabe Peers" seeking power and "Pawns" seeking personal gain at the expense of the "Commons".

Dismantling this fourth branch of government must be done carefully and any necessary functions preserved. Functions and powers that present the greatest threat to our freedom must go first.

A basic tenet of our law was that the accused was innocent until proven guilty in a court of law. This started to change with the "HEPBURN ACT OF 1906". Congress gave the Interstate Commerce Commission (ICC) the power to set railroad freight rates that were "reasonable and just" (after a full hearing) and placed the "burden of proof" on the accused (the railroads). To undo the ICC's decision, the railroads had to prove in court that the ICC was wrong (the railroads were guilty until proven innocent). Congress has continued to increase the power of the bureaucracy since that time.

The police must have "probable cause" and obtain a warrant from the judicial branch to go into an accused criminal's home and search for evidence. The bureaucrat only has to walk into the "Commons" business and demand access and cooperation. The accused criminal has more rights than the "Commons" (producer). Bureaucrats (from several agencies) can enter and investigate a business without "probable cause" or a warrant. The bureaucrats have the power to levy fines for what they consider infractions of their regulations. If the "Wannabe Peers" want to pressure a "Common" and the bureaucrats fail to find an infraction, they can create new regulations that are sure to be violated, giving the "Wannabe Peers" the leverage needed to extort support or control the actions of the "Commons". To create new regulations, the bureaucrats might be inconvenienced by having to hold a "public hearing", causing a slight delay and giving the bureaucrat another excuse to increase their budget. The new regulations can be swiftly enforced and the "Commons" destroyed, while the "Wannabe Peers" and their "Pawns" feed on the corpse. If the disaster caused by the bureaucrats becomes public knowledge, the "Wannabe Peers" can always condemn the "out of control bureaucrats" and gain political support by promising to correct the problem.

The fourth branch of the government must go the way of the Dodo[39] bird if we are to regain our freedom! The bureaucracy must be incrementally stripped of power until it becomes irrelevant and can be eliminated. The action to provide the "Commons" with relief from the oppression of each agency should be in the following order:

- The most dangerous power of the bureaucracy is the ability to levy fines. That power would be replaced with the requirement that infractions that could not be resolved by negotiation between the agency and the "Commons" be referred to the Justice Department for prosecution. The "Commons" would retain the "presumption of innocence" until convicted in a court of law. How quaint, giving the "Commons" the same rights as an accused criminal!

- The power to enter a business without consent of the business would be the next to be deleted. The bureaucrat would be required to obtain a warrant to enter the premises if access is denied. "Probable Cause" of an infraction would be required to obtain the warrant. More equality between the "Commons" and the accused criminal!

- The bureaucrat's "conflict of interest" in proposing new regulations must be recognized and neutralized. The bureaucracy's prime objective is to increase its budget – new regulations support a budget increase. The bureaucrats would not be allowed to either propose or create new regulations.

- Each agency would be required to submit to Congress a detailed "Economic Impact Statement" on each active regulation.

- The "Economic Impact Statement" would be prepared by independent economists not affiliated with the bureaucracy.

- Each "Economic Impact Statement" would be subject to independent review prior to submission to Congress.

- The regulation would be abolished 90 days after the "Economic Impact Statement" was submitted to Congress. To continue the regulation, Congress would have to approve the ""Economic Impact Statement" and write the regulation into law.

- A detailed "Economic Impact Statement" approved by Congress would be required before Congress could even vote on any new law.

- Periodic reviews of all laws that affect the economy would be required, complete with "**Economic Impact Statements**". The failure of Congress to approve the review within 90 days would repeal the law.

- Transfer the power to prosecute and investigate infractions to the Justice Department.

Once these steps were completed, the agency would be irrelevant and could be abolished. The "Wannabe Peers" will be quick to point out that congressional committees study the legislation so an "Economic Impact Statement" is not necessary. History shows that the Congressional committee has not protected the "Commons" or our individual freedom. Congress could not blame the bureaucracy for the failure of the bureaucrat's policies and the requirement for an "Economic Impact Statement" would prevent Congress from claiming ignorance of the consequences of legislative action or passing a law with unknown content. Approval of an "Economic Impact Statement" prior to voting on the legislation would prevent the congressional leadership from passing legislation that has unknown provisions.

THE INCOME TAX:

Once the "Wannabe Peers'" use of the IRS to punish political dissenters has been eliminated, some of the support for the income tax may disappear. However, the income tax is a terrible drain on the economy and increasing poverty is a necessary part of the Wannabe Peers'" strategy. In addition to making it more difficult to obtain capital to fund new projects, the cost[64] (2004) to corporations of complying with IRS regulations was almost 25 percent of the tax paid. Since 2004 much complexity has been added to the income tax regulations, so the 25 percent figure is probably significantly understated for today's economy. This means that compliance with the IRS regulations causes corporations to expend non-productive labor with an average value of at least 25 percent of the income tax paid. This is an average figure and the compliance cost (as a percent of taxes) would be much more for small growing companies with little or no profit. For a start-up company the compliance cost is a nonproductive expense that increases the cost of doing business. Of course, this cost must be passed on to the consumer. The compliance cost for IRS regulations is a direct assault on the "technology dividend". The income tax must be replaced with a more equitable tax system to allow growth of the technology dividend and achieve the prosperity that capitalism can provide.

EARMARKS:

The requirement that Congress approve an "Economic Impact Statement" before it could pass a new law should end the "Earmark" problem.

INFLATION:

Once the inflation of currency is recognized as a tax, the required "Economic Impact Statement" on the Federal budget should solve the inflation problem. If the long term inflation of the currency were equal to the growth of the "technology dividend", a stable value to the dollar would be achieved.

SHERMAN ANTITRUST ACT:

It is virtually impossible to determine the economic damage that has resulted from the Sherman Antitrust act. It should be repealed immediately. The elimination of the bureaucracy will only add small inconveniences to the "Wannabe Peers" enforcement of the antitrust laws. As soon as the "fourth branch of government" is eliminated, repeal of the Antitrust Laws would be the next priority. The ability of the "Wannabe Peers" to protect politically powerful but "technologically challenged" political supporters from innovators and punish successful "Commons" must be ended. Prosperity demands that the "technology dividend" be set free from the "emergency brake" applied by the Sherman Antitrust Act.

Repealing the Antitrust Laws will not be easy. The "Wannabe Peers" will warn of the dangers of an economic monopoly. The truth is that a monopoly has never had an extended life unless it was supported by the use of force and the government has the monopoly on force. An effective tactic might be to apply the Antitrust Laws to government enforced monopolies. The post office, labor unions and public education certainly violate the Sherman Antitrust Act and would be prime targets. However, the labor unions are specifically exempted from the Antitrust Act. These three examples have a much more detrimental effect on the consumer than a company like Microsoft adding features to its product that limit competitors' ability to sell that feature. The purpose of the tactic is not to actually apply the law to these monopolies. The purpose is to repeal the Sherman Antitrust Law.

OTHER GOVERNMENT ABUSES TO INDIVIDUAL LIBERTY:

Victimless crimes[71] are laws that attempt to control individual behavior but do not create a victim when the crime is violated. Examples are controlled substances laws, laws against prostitution and public decency. These "victimless crimes" have a tremendous economic cost. According to Peter McWilliams' book, "AIN'T NOBODY'S BUSINESS IF YOU DO", over 350,000 people are incarcerated for "victimless crimes" and 1,500,000 more are on parole or probation, their earning capacity forever diminished by a felony conviction. $50 billion will be spent to punish victimless crime offenses and $150 billion will be lost in tax revenue. The cost to the economy is probably much greater than the estimates. Some estimates show that fully one-third of the United State's agricultural GDP[72] is marijuana, an illegal substance. The cost to the economy is staggering. The cost in human misery is even greater. Would ending the recreational use of marijuana and other drugs be desirable? Perhaps, but it is not the government's decision. It is the individual's decision. Did we learn nothing from the experiment with prohibition? The cure is worse than the disease. "Victimless crimes" destroy wealth and increase poverty and that increases the "Wannabe Peers" constituency. So don't expect any help on changing the "victimless crime" laws from the "Wannabe Peers". The consequences of the "victimless crime" laws advance the "Wannabe Peers'" agenda.

GOVERNMENT AND THE EMPLOYER AND EMPLOYEE RELATIONSHIP:

Governmental meddling in the relationship between the employer and employee increases the cost of all "consumable assets" and "active assets". This meddling is simply an attempt by the "Wannabe Peers" to obtain political support from powerful pressure groups and "Pawns" by using the government's monopoly on force to redistribute wealth at a terrible cost to the economy and individual freedom. A complete evaluation of the cost and injustice caused by the government's intrusion into the relationship between the employer and employee would fill a book of its own. The requirement for an "Economic Impact Statement" might eliminate this problem.

ENVIRONMENTAL REGULATIONS:

Environmental regulations based upon emotional arguments with no basis in fact and total disregard for the economic consequences have had a devastating effect on the economy. The destruction of wealth by many current regulations pale when compared to the economic consequences of using government force to limit carbon dioxide emissions. Serious consideration has never been given to a program that has more potential to:

- Reduce individual freedom.

116

- Destroy more wealth.
- Redistribute more wealth to the "Wannabe Peers" and their supporters.
- Create more poverty and increase the "Wannabe Peers'" constituency.

The bogus claim[6, 7] that carbon dioxide emissions cause "global warming" is supported only by emotional claims of disaster if we don't act immediately. No valid proof is offered that carbon dioxide emissions have any effect on climate change.

The "**Energy Alchemist**" touting "alternative energy" won't tell you that the difference between "alternative energy" and "primary energy" is that "alternative energy" costs more. Remember, all "consumable assets" have energy content. Any increase in the cost of energy increases the cost of living and creates poverty. The increase in the cost of living due to elimination or reduction of carbon dioxide emissions will make almost everyone dependent upon the government for subsistence. Without carbon dioxide emissions, the government will have little to distribute.

The cost of "alternative energy", touted by the **"Energy Alchemist"** will be devastating to the consumer and create wide spread poverty at levels we never dreamed of, even in the "great depression". The destruction of the economy, resulting from elimination or reduction of carbon dioxide emissions will surely produce the "Wannabe Peers" final objective, the "economic crisis" that gives them total control. Even those who expect to profit from the elimination of carbon dioxide emissions will find that the wealth received by virtue of this attack on civilization has little or no value.

Many books[6, 7] have been written on this subject and more are being written today. The subject is fully documented. There is no need for more discussion on this subject in this book.

Government coerced loans:

For over fifteen years, the Government has interfered in the home mortgage business forcing lenders to lower credit requirements. Lenders were induced to make loans to persons not capable of repaying those loans. This ill advised and little understood program is the cause of the economic crisis of 2008 and the home building boom that preceded it. This crisis was caused by the blatant use of implied government force to redistribute wealth from the lender to the borrower. However, it was the ordinary citizens, you, who were stuck with the bill and the misery it created. Wholesale destruction of wealth was the ultimate result. From the "Wannabe Peers" point of view, this was a highly successful program that significantly increased poverty and the "Wannabe Peers'" constituency.

There are many other programs similar to the ones mentioned above and the five programs that were analyzed in chapter 5. There is no need to bore the reader with more specifics. If the people will embrace individual freedom, the violating programs will be identified and eliminated.

SUMMARY AND CONCLUSIONS:

This book has proven conclusively that the "Wannabe Peers'" programs:

- Destroy wealth
- Inhibit the creation of wealth
- Create poverty and misery for the masses
- Destroy individual freedom
- Increase the "Wannabe Peers" constituency

The "Wannabe Peers" claim that the only solution to problems created by their programs is more government regulations and surrender of more of our individual freedom. The "preponderance of propaganda" has convinced many "Pawns" and pressure groups of the success of their programs. The illogical proposal that the only solution to problems created by the loss of our freedom is to surrender more of our freedom has received wide acceptance. The "Wannabe Peers" are very close to creating the economic crisis that will create a Totalitarian government in America. Just as an economic crisis brought tyrants to power in Italy and Germany, just as Cuba's revolution failed to restore freedom, the "Wannabe Peers" can gain control of America. There will be no United States left to save the world!

History has demonstrated that the "Wannabe Peers" have used the power of the bureaucracy to prosecute and punish dissenters and there is no reason to believe that the current crop of "Wannabe Peers" is any more moral than those of the past. Regaining our lost freedoms will be a dangerous undertaking, but the only alternative is the misery, abject poverty and mediocrity created by a Totalitarian government. Just as the "Minutemen" faced King George III's English Regulars on Lexington Green, we are facing hoards of bureaucrats, backed by the "Wannabe Peers". Will you stand up to the "Wannabe Peers" as the "Minutemen" stood up to King George III or will you sink into the mediocrity of a Totalitarian world?

IS THIS STILL THE "HOME OF THE BRAVE"?

THE END!

OR IS IT A NEW BEGINNING?

IT IS UP TO YOU!

<u>GOD BLESS AMERICA</u>

BIBLIOGRAPHY

1 Wikipedia Encyclopedia, Prohibition in the United States
http://en.wikipedia.org/wiki/Prohibition_in_the_United_States

2 Wikipedia encyclopedia
http://en.wikipedia.org/wiki/Erie_Canal#Proposal_and_logistics

3 Ayn Rand's philosophy www.aynrand.org

4 Wikipedia encyclopedia List of countries by GDP (nominal)
http://en.wikipedia.org/wiki/List_of_countries_by_GDP_(nominal

5 MEASURING WORTH U. S. GROSS DOMESTIC PRODUCT . http://www.measuringworth.org/usgdp/

6 "CLIMATE CONFUSION" Roy W. Spencer, ENCOUNTER BOOKS, NEW YORK

7 COMMONSENSE21C.COM - climate change page
http://commonsense21c.com/CLIMATE.html

8 G.I.BILL
http://en.wikipedia.org/wiki/G._I._Bill#After_World_War_II

9 PROMETHEUS
http://en.wikipedia.org/wiki/Prometheus

10 INDUSTRIAL REVOLUTION Wikipedia encyclopedia
http://en.wikipedia.org/wiki/Industrial_Revolution/history

11 STEAM ENGINE Wikipedia encyclopedia
http://en.wikipedia.org/wiki/Steam_engine#History

12   Wikipedia encyclopedia early government charity
Tenth Century http://en.wikipedia.org/wiki/Almshouse

13   Wikipedia encyclopedia – quote from JOHN
DALBERG   http://en.wikipedia.org/wiki/John_Dalberg-
Acton,_1st_Baron_Acton#.22Lord_Acton.27s_dictum.22

14   Quote attributed to George Santayana (1863?-
1952), U.S. philosopher, poet.
http://plato.stanford.edu/entries/santayana/   Center for
the Study of Language and Information, Stanford University,
Stanford, CA 94305

15   Benito Amilcare Andrea Mussolini
Wikipedia Encyclopedia
http://en.wikipedia.org/wiki/Mussolini MACROHISTORY AND
WORLD REPORT
http://www.fsmitha.com/h2/ch12.htmhttp://gi.grolier.com/
wwii/wwii_mussolini.html
http://www.newworldencyclopedia.org/entry/Benito_Mussoli
ni#Early_Years

16   Adolf Hitler, The Life of Adolf Hitler
http://www.adolfhitler.dk/
http://en.wikipedia.org/wiki/Hitler
MACROHISTORY AND WORLD REPORT
http://www.fsmitha.com/h2/ch13.htm
http://www.fsmitha.com/h2/ch16.htm
http://www.fsmitha.com/h2/ch21b.html
       Sturmabteilung
http://en.wikipedia.org/wiki/Sturmabteilung
       SS or Schutzstaffel
http://encarta.msn.com/encyclopedia_761586855/SS.html
       "LIFE OF ADOLF HITLER"
http://www.adolfhitler.dk/
       NEW WORLD ENCYCLOPEDIA
http://www.newworldencyclopedia.org/entry/Hitler

SPARTACUS EDUCATIONAL
http://www.spartacus.schoolnet.co.uk/GERsa.htm

17   Fidel Alejandro Castro Ruz Wikipedia Encyclopedia,
http://en.wikipedia.org/wiki/Fidel_Castro   Answers.com -
http://www.answers.com/topic/fidel-castro MACROHISTORY
AND WORLD REPORT
http://www.fsmitha.com/h2/ch24t63.html

18   GEORGE WASHINGTON
http://encarta.msn.com/encyclopedia_761564084_7/George_
Washington.html

19   BENJAMIN FRANKLIN
http://www.wisdomquotes.com/000974.html

20   JORDON, JOHN STEEL *AN EMPIRE OF WEALTH"*
NEW YORK, HARPERCOLLINS PUBLISHERS INC.
21 MAGNA CARTA - Wikipedia encyclopedia
http://en.wikipedia.org/wiki/Magna_Carta

22   SILVER CONTENT OF ROMAN COINS:
http://en.wikipedia.org/wiki/Roman_coinage#Further_histor
y_of_Roman_coins

23   HISTORY OF METALWORKING:
http://www.bloodandsawdust.com/sca/lathes.html

24   SHERMAN ANTITRUST ACT:
http://everything2.com/index.pl?node_id=548896
http://en.wikipedia.org/wiki/Sherman_Anti_Trust_Act
http://topics.law.cornell.edu/wex/Antitrust
http://www.cato.org/pubs/journal/cj9n3/cj9n3-13.pdf
http://www.cato.org/pubs/handbook/hb105-39.html
http://en.wikipedia.org/wiki/Alan_Greenspan
http://www.fsmitha.com/h3/h46-am.htm

25   LEXINGTON GREEN
http://en.wikipedia.org/wiki/Lexington_Green

http://www.newworldencyclopedia.org/entry/Battles_of_Lexington_and_Concord

26 CONSTITUTIONAL CONVENTION
http://en.wikipedia.org/wiki/Philadelphia_Convention
http://en.wikipedia.org/wiki/Timeline_of_the_United_States_Constitution

27 MANIFEST DESTINY
http://en.wikipedia.org/wiki/Manifest_Destiny
http://www.newworldencyclopedia.org/entry/Manifest_Destiny

28 SUFFRAGE
http://en.wikipedia.org/wiki/Voting_and_elections

29 PROPAGANDA
http://www.newworldencyclopedia.org/entry/Propaganda

30 The Divine Right ofKINGS
http://www.newworldencyclopedia.org/entry/Divine_right_of_kings

31 PATRICK HENRY
http://en.wikipedia.org/wiki/Patrick_Henry

32 RONALD REAGAN
http://en.wikipedia.org/wiki/Ronald_Reagan

33 Standard Oil:
http://www.bookrags.com/wiki/Standard_Oil
http://en.wikipedia.org/wiki/Standard_Oil
http://en.citizendium.org/wiki/Standard_Oil
http://www.reference.com/browse/Standard+Oil+Company?jss=1 http://www.theobjectivestandard.com/issues/2008-summer/standard-oil-company.asp
http://books.google.com/books?id=aIIEAAAAMAAJ&pg=PA1&dq=intitle:standard+intitle:oil&num=30&as_brr=1#PPA1,M1

34 NOTHERN SECURITIES COMPANY ANTITRUST
http://en.wikipedia.org/wiki/Northern_Securities_Company
35 "FDR and the IRS" by Burton W. Folsom, Jr.
Prepared for the Durell Colloquium," The Role of Markets and
Governments in Pursuing the Common Good," at Hillsdale
College, October 28, 2006.

36 Sbardellati, John.
*"Power to Destroy: The Political Uses of the IRS from Kennedy to
Nixon"*

37 "The Lawless State: The Crimes of the U. S.
Intelligence Agencies" by Morton H. Halperin (Author), Jerry J.
Berman (Author), Robert L. Borosage (Author), Christine M.
Marwick

38 HYPERINFLATION:
http://www.newworldencyclopedia.org/entry/Weimar_Repu
blic http://en.wikipedia.org/wiki/Hyperinflation

39 DODO BIRD:
http://en.wikipedia.org/wiki/Dodo_(bird)

40 "THE ENABLING ACT OF 1933":
http://en.wikipedia.org/wiki/Enabling_Act_(Germany)

41 IRA TARBELL
http://en.wikipedia.org/wiki/Ida_Tarbell
http://www.bookrags.com/biography/ida-minerva-tarbell/
"THE HISTORY OF THE Standard Oil COMPANY" (New
York, NY: McClure, Philips & Company 1904) pp. 36-37

42 ECONOMY OF SCALE:
http://en.wikipedia.org/wiki/Economy_of_scale

43 JOHN D. ROCKEFELLER:
http://en.wikipedia.org/wiki/John_D._Rockefeller
http://www.bgsu.edu/departments/acs/1890s/rockefeller/bi
o2.htm http://en.wikipedia.org/wiki/Allan_Nevins

44 ROBBER BARONS:
http://en.wikipedia.org/wiki/Robber_baron_(industrialist)

45 ALLEN NEVINS
http://en.wikipedia.org/wiki/Allan_Nevins

46 INFLATION RATE 1914-PRESENT:
http://inflationdata.com/Inflation/Inflation_Rate/HistoricalInflation.aspx

47 THOMAS PAINE:
http://en.wikipedia.org/wiki/Thomas_Paine%27s_Common_Sense

48 INTERSTATE COMMERCE COMMISSION:
http://en.wikipedia.org/wiki/Interstate_Commerce_Commission http://en.wikipedia.org/wiki/Regulatory_capture
http://www.pbs.org/wgbh/amex/streamliners/peopleevents/e_ica.html
JORDON, JOHN STEEL *"AN EMPIRE OF WEALTH"* NEW YORK, HARPERCOLLINS PUBLISHERS INC.
http://encarta.msn.com/encyclopedia_761572204/Government_Regulation_of_Railroads.html
http://www.american-rails.com/railroading-in-the-1930s.html
http://www.history.com/encyclopedia.do?articleId=220264
http://www.aar.org/PubCommon/Documents/AboutTheIndustry/Overview.pdf

49 GOVERNMENT FAILURE
http://en.wikipedia.org/wiki/Government_failure

50 "IRON TRIANGLE"
http://en.wikipedia.org/wiki/Iron_triangle
http://www.auburn.edu/~johnspm/gloss/iron_triangles

51 GOVERNMENT AGENCYS
http://en.wikipedia.org/wiki/Independent_agencies_of_the_U
nited_States_government

52 WOODROW WILSON - The New Freedom: A Call For the Emancipation of the Generous Energies of a People - PUBLISHER BIBLIOBAZAAR

53 "REGULATORY CAPTURE"
http://en.wikipedia.org/wiki/Regulatory_capture

54 EARMARKS:
http://en.wikipedia.org/wiki/Earmark_(politics)
        http://earmarks.omb.gov/2008_appropriations_earmar
ks_110th_congress.html
        http://www.measuringworth.org/usgdp/
http://en.wikipedia.org/wiki/U.S._population

55 inflation calculator:
        http://www.westegg.com/inflation/
http://www.halfhill.com/inflation.html
http://www.moneychimp.com/articles/econ/inflation_calcula
tor.htm http://www.bls.gov/data/inflation_calculator.htm

56 OVERVIEW OF AMERICA'S FREIGHT RAILROADS
http://www.aar.org/PubCommon/Documents/AboutTheIndu
stry/Overview.pdf

57 FEDERAL RESERVE SYSTEM:
http://www.federalreserve.gov/aboutthefed/default.htm
        http://www.federalreserveeducation.org/fed101/histo
ry/ http://en.wikipedia.org/wiki/Federal_Reserve_System

58 PRICE OF GOLD
http://www.finfacts.ie/Private/curency/goldmarketprice.htm

59 PRICE OF SILVER
http://www.goldmastersusa.com/silver_historical_prices.asp

60   GREENBACK:
http://ecclesia.org/forum/uploads/bondservant/greenbackP.
pdf

61   INFLATION DATA:
http://inflationdata.com/inflation/Inflation_Rate/HistoricalIn
flation.aspx?dsInflation_currentPage=7
http://www.nowandfutures.com/key_stats.html

62   INFLATION:
http://wordnetweb.princeton.edu/perl/webwn?s=inflation

63   INCOME TAX
http://en.wikipedia.org/wiki/History_of_Income_Taxation_in_
the_United_States#Income_tax
http://www.ntu.org/main/page.php?PageID=19

64   COMPLEXITY AND COST OF TAX CODE
http://74.125.47.132/search?q=cache:MgroUVPv3W4J:www.t
axfoundation.org/files/sr138.pdf+cost+of+complying+with+c
operate+income+tax&cd=1&hl=en&ct=clnk&gl=us

65   TESTIMONY OF DAVID BURNHAM ON IRS ABUSES
(testimony before a Senate committee)
http://famguardian.org/TaxFreedom/Evidence/Congressiona
l/DavidBurnhamTestimony.htm

66   Lyndon Johnson, the IRS and churches
http://www.gather.com/viewArticle.action?articleId=281474
977666190

67   PERCENT OF POPULATION WORKING IN
AGRICULTURE
http://www.ers.usda.gov/publications/eib3/eib3.htm

68   WANNABE PEERS USE OF THE IRS 1977-PRESENT
http://www.wnd.com/news/article.asp?ARTICLE_ID=14702
http://www.papillonsartpalace.com/churches.htm
http://www.judicialwatch.org/printer_2371.shtml

http://www.judicialwatch.org/1737.shtml
http://www.fieldwerks.com/bush.htm
http://www.democraticunderground.com/discuss/duboard.p
hp?az=view_all&address=110x10771
http://eatatjoesplace.blogspot.com/2005/11/president-
bushs-war-on-people-of-faith.html

69 IRS REFORM 1998
http://www.washingtonpost.com/wp-
srv/politics/special/tax/stories/irs072398.htm

70 CLINTON'S ENEMIES AND THE IRS
http://archive.newsmax.com/archives/articles/2002/4/22/2
00136.shtml

71 VICTIMLESS CRIMES – LIBRARY OF HALEXANDRIA:
http://www.halexandria.org/dward267.htm
"AIN'T NOBODY'S BUSINESS IF YOU DO" book by Peter
McWilliams

72 MARIJUANA – % OF U.S. AGRICULTURAL GDP
http://www.drugscience.org/Archive/bcr2/cashcrops.html

BOOKS BY FELTON WILLIAMSON JR. AKA "TOBY"

"21ST CENTURY COMMON SENSE"

"COMMON SENSE – THE WAY BACK"

TO LEARN MORE ABOUT THESE BOOKS THESE BOOKS GO TO
"commonsense21c.com"

THESE BOOKS CAN BE PURCHASED FROM LINKS ON
"commonsense21c.com"
Or
AMAZON.COM